THE LAST DAYS OF THE CONFEDERACY IN NORTHEAST GEORGIA

THE LAST DAYS OF THE CONFEDERACY IN NORTHEAST GEORGIA

RAY CHANDLER

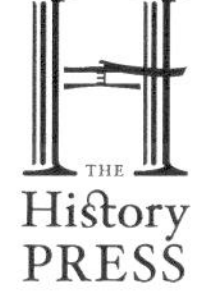

Published by The History Press
Charleston, SC 29403
www.historypress.net

Front cover image: *The Last Council of War* by Wilbur Kurtz. Kurtz's painting is owned by and on display at the Burt-Stark Mansion in the city of Abbeville, South Carolina. The painting depicts the last meeting Confederate president Jefferson Davis had with his war council before the end of the Civil War. The meeting took place at the mansion in Abbeville. Afterward, Davis fled to northeast Georgia. *Courtesy of the City of Abbeville. Image taken by College of Charleston Special Collections.*

First published 2015

Manufactured in the United States

ISBN 978.1.62619.344.4

Library of Congress Control Number: 2015931112

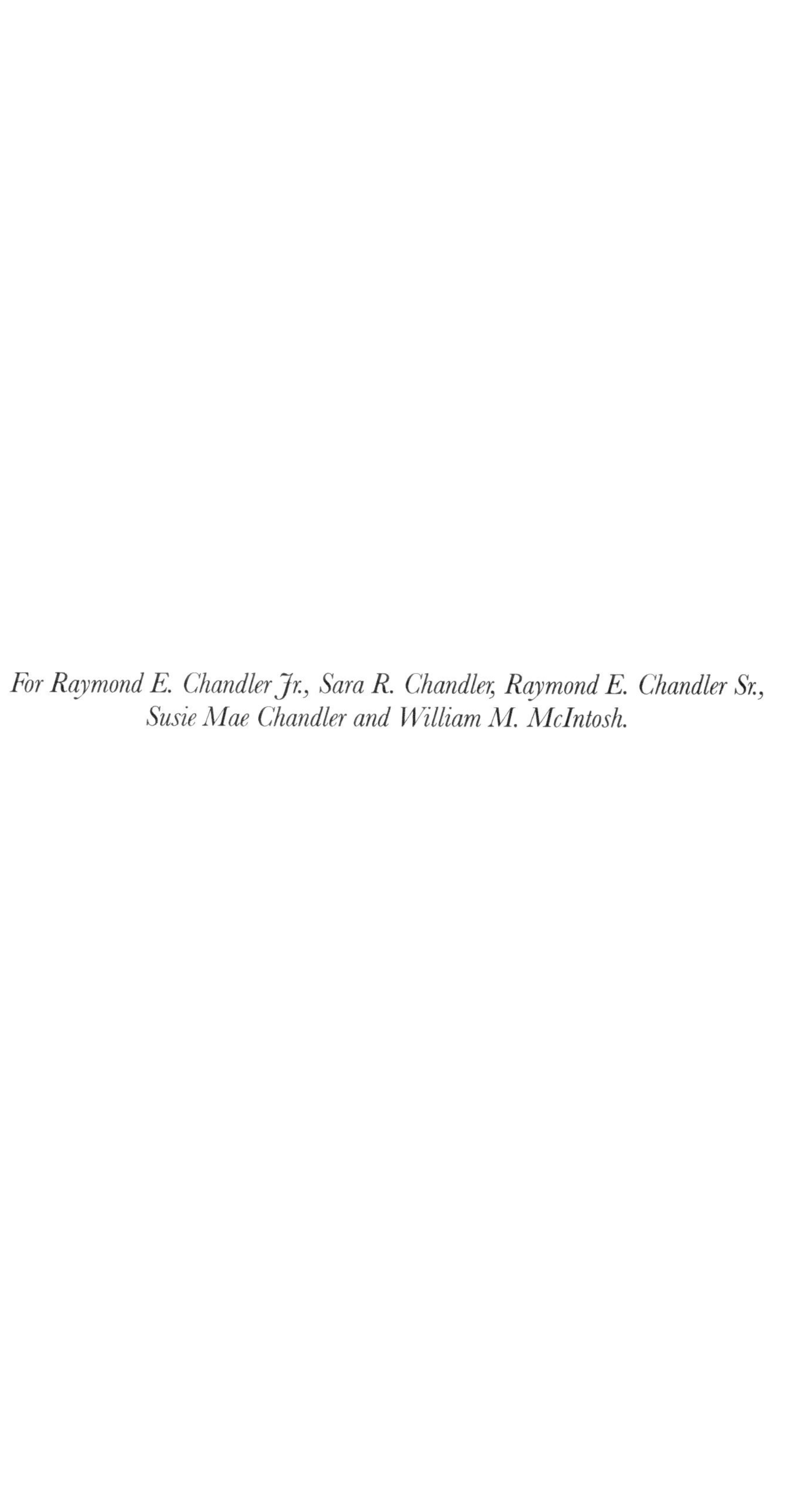

For Raymond E. Chandler Jr., Sara R. Chandler, Raymond E. Chandler Sr., Susie Mae Chandler and William M. McIntosh.

Contents

Preface

The scene that begins the first chapter of this book has haunted me for years. The tableau of Colonel William McPherson McIntosh, commander of the Fifteenth Georgia Infantry, sitting in his tent, writing to his son his thoughts on soldiering and the war in which the colonel found himself is a dramatist's dream, yet it actually happened, no doubt in the same way it happened in untold other instances from which no letters survived. The son was eager to get into the fray, no doubt inspired by dreams of glory and by the pageantry he had witnessed when his father and others had gone off to war. The father's response to the son's dreams are those nearly all fathers would make, once the father himself had drunk deep from the well the young man yearned for. What makes it especially poignant to me are two things. The first is knowing the colonel's own fate, which will be related later. The second is that he was my great-great-uncle.

In my family, as in many families in the South up through at least my own generation (I was born in 1962), the Civil War was always more than something we read of in history books. We heard the stories told by older people who, in many cases, would have been told them by people who had lived through the war. Some were family stories of glory and such, as about William McIntosh and the other William in the family, William H. Mattox, my maternal great-great-grandfather, who had also served in the Fifteenth Georgia. Both were tragic figures. McIntosh was a hero. Mattox's tragedy was that he wasn't. Some stories were funny, such as that of David Chandler, my paternal great-great-grandfather. Too old to serve in the army, he had been sheriff of Jackson County, Georgia, for a time during the war, and the story of his encounter with a band of Union cavalry, probably some of Stoneman's men, always brought a chuckle at every retelling. Other tales brought more somber reflection, such as of my maternal great-grandmother remembering, when a little girl, standing in a cotton field and hearing the explosions and seeing the rising smoke as the Confederate army evacuated Atlanta. Each story, in its own way, added our family's brushstrokes, however small, to the panoramic portrait of the war.

There were also the stories about the famous local characters who had walked the same ground as we and had played their own parts in the war. For example, Alexander H. Stephens and Robert A. Toombs had both made names for themselves locally, practicing law in the northern judicial circuit before gaining their state and national political stature. Stephens was the reluctant Confederate, against secession yet embracing the cause of state's rights. He served as vice-president of the Confederacy and had spent a good part of the war in Georgia, on the outs with the Confederate national government. Toombs, from Washington, in Wilkes County, just south of Elbert County, is to me the most interesting of all. Blustering, bombastic, hard-drinking—in fact, often drunk—Bob Toombs. A brilliant intellect trapped in a soul that could govern neither its temperament nor its passions, ultimately a tragic figure worthy of an ancient Grecian playwright. Perhaps no other man in Georgia so embodied the time and the place, and the passions and the ambitions that led Georgia out of the Union. Indeed, a lot of speeches were given in favor of secession at the November 1860 debate in the Milledgeville statehouse, but perhaps Toombs's roaring best summed up the reasons why enough Georgian voters, even those who initially opposed secession, ultimately gave a slim overall winning margin in support of Southern independence.

And of course there were the enduring stories surrounding the Confederate treasury and its strange odyssey under the guard of adolescent Confederate naval midshipmen that ended, at least in part, in Washington when the fleeing Jefferson Davis had his last cabinet meeting in a building on the square and dissolved his government before continuing his flight from Federal forces. The Confederate treasury can be accounted for, but what can't is part of the gold and silver belonging to the banks of Richmond that traveled with the treasury for much of the time. Tales of buried treasure stemming from a raid by some renegade Kentucky cavalrymen abound to this day. All of these—the historic figures who had tread the same ground as we, the events that had played out practically in our backyards—made the war far more than mere history. The sweeping histories of the war told of great campaigns, bloody battles, glorious victories and glorious defeats. A piece of these were ours, but our local history was ours alone.

One could argue on solid ground, I think, that Georgia's secession was essential to the Confederacy's very formation and life. Its railroads, its burgeoning industrial base and its keystone location linking the upper southern Atlantic coastal states to the heart of the cotton belt in the Gulf Coast states—all of these were essential to any chance for the new nation's survival. Not without reason, after all, is Sherman's campaign through Georgia considered by some the deciding struggle of the war.

One could also argue, I think, that without the Georgian leaders who hailed from the northeast corner of Georgia—Bob Toombs; the Cobb brothers of Athens, Howell and Thomas R.R.; and Georgia's governor in 1860 and throughout the war, Joseph E. Brown—there would have been no secession. The fierce determination of these men to see Georgia leave the Union translated into political theater on a grand scale. Others played their parts, but these four, not always allies before the war, were the producers, directors and principal actors. They were able to overcome the initial deficit of popular support for secession and the skilled rhetoric of Alexander Stephens and other opponents. They won by dint of rhetoric that flew high and low, appealing to Georgians' highest notions of self-determined liberty as well as to their most horrible fears: former slaves freed and running amok and, even worse, seeking retribution.

So war came, but it did not really come home to northeast Georgia in the way it did to other areas of the South until the very last months and days. Before that, when the residents saw a man in Union blue, he was a prisoner. And it is this story I set out to tell. It is a story I have wanted to tell as completely as possible for over thirty years. I have told it in bits and pieces and now want to put as much of it together as possible for the first time. It can't be told in its entirety, not in one book, but I hope to tell enough to do justice to the people written about. (In the case of William Mattox, that involves telling the truth about a genuine scoundrel whose genes I do indeed carry.)

Wherever possible and as much as practicable, I have let the characters tell their own stories. Now nearly into my third decade as a working journalist, I've learned that one can add perspective, but for the most color and savor, let the people speak for themselves. As Mark Twain once put it, "Don't say that an old lady screamed. Bring her on and let her scream."

There are many to be thanked here. First, The History Press for allowing me the opportunity to produce this book. Second, to Olin Jackson, who gave me my start in published historical writing in the pages of what was first *North Georgia Journal* and later *Georgia Backroads* magazine. And third to Daniel Roper, who after taking over from Olin kept me writing. Most of all, my parents, who from my earliest age kept my appetite for history well fed. The first family vacation I recall, in fact, was to Charleston, South Carolina, including a visit to Fort Sumter. There were many more exciting places to come.

If I have one hope from this, it is that anyone reading it comes to know the joys of loving history.

Ray Chandler
June 2014
Elberton, Georgia

Chapter 1
"...This Thing of Soldiering..."

The night of May 30, 1862, in camp on the Confederate lines near the Chickahominy River. Colonel William McPherson McIntosh, commander of the Fifteenth Georgia Infantry, sat alone in his tent, bent over his field desk in the glow of a lantern. The rains of the past few days had stopped, and the word was that the next day and the days after would bring action. Already, McIntosh could hear the sound of artillery farther up the line.[1]

The Army of Northern Virginia under General Joseph Johnston lay arrayed this night facing the larger Union Army of the Potomac under General George McClellan in what promised to be a death struggle for the Confederate capital of Richmond, just a few miles west. Mile by mile, the Confederates had fought a fighting retreat up the peninsula between the York and James Rivers before the slow Union advance until there wasn't much farther they could back up. The glory of the heady days of the Confederates' victory at First Manassas the previous July had frayed as steadily as men's nerves over the winter's skirmishing and now seemed a distant memory for the men who had been there.[2]

McIntosh had still been in Georgia as the smoke had lifted over Manassas. The Fifteenth Georgia was just taking form, and McIntosh, a major then, was learning something of soldiering. The drill field version of soldiering, that is, the marching in new uniforms, under fluttering flags, to spirited fifes and drums, assured you were marching to victory. In Virginia, the men had found the mud and disease of camp life over a cold, Virginia winter, in

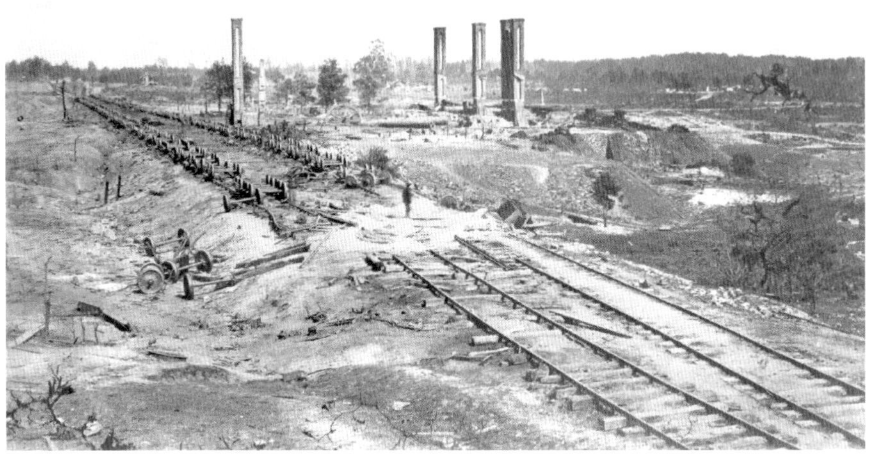

The path of destruction left by Sherman's army near Atlanta. The northeast corner of Georgia was spared this hard hand of the war.

addition to the normal dangers of war. An outbreak of measles in the fall of 1861—a common consequence of so many men from so many different areas thrown together in one place—had decimated the ranks, at one point reducing the Fifteenth Georgia to about half strength. Indeed, the measles outbreak had been in part responsible for McIntosh rising to the regiment's command. The commanding colonel, Thomas W. Thomas, a judge on the North Georgia circuit in civilian life, had resigned after measles had left him weakened. The lieutenant colonel, Linton Stephens, half brother of Confederate vice president Alexander H. Stephens, had also resigned in the same condition. So, too, had McIntosh's twenty-six-year-old brother-in-law, William Henry Mattox, a captain, not from measles but from a host of general camp ailments.[3]

The colonel left no record of his thoughts on soldiering in the heady days of 1860 and early 1861, but if they bubbled with dreams of glory and easy victory, those had fallen flat. It was his experience that McIntosh now set out to convey to his seventeen-year-old son, Singleton, a student at Georgia Military Institute in Marietta, near Atlanta. The young man was itching to leave school and join the army, the colonel had learned, but he could not see the boy a soldier:

This is natural, considering your age, and, I must say, patriotic. But I have no idea that it is best for yourselves, or, for your country...You have not the remotest idea of the trials, hardships and difficulties which camp life would expose you to, but you could endure all these things if you should keep your health...Yet you can by no means count on that here...If you expect pleasure, by coming into the Army, you will be greatly deceived. Thousands have gone out with that expectation and are now disappointed. This thing of soldiering looks better from a distance than it does close by.[4]

The "thing of soldiering" began for McIntosh on a bright, sunny day in late May 1861, when he had marched at the head of the McIntosh Volunteers, a company he had raised and partially equipped. His youngest son, four-year-old James, dressed in a mock Zouave uniform and beating on a drum, led off the procession of his father's company as well as three others—the Bowman Guards, the Fireside Guards and the Goshen Blues—that had marched through Elberton on their way to the wagons that would haul them to the railroad. Crowds cheered from the sidewalks and perches atop buildings around the square. Except for the Goshen Blues, which would end up in the Thirty-eighth Georgia, all would become part of the Fifteenth Georgia once they arrived in Atlanta.[5]

The forty-six-year-old McIntosh had been a lawyer in civilian life, one of the most prominent in his hometown, Elberton, practicing at one time with his brother-in-law, Young L.G. Harris, who had later become a powerful judge in nearby Athens, in Clarke County. McIntosh also owned an eight-hundred-acre plantation in eastern Elbert County, rich land

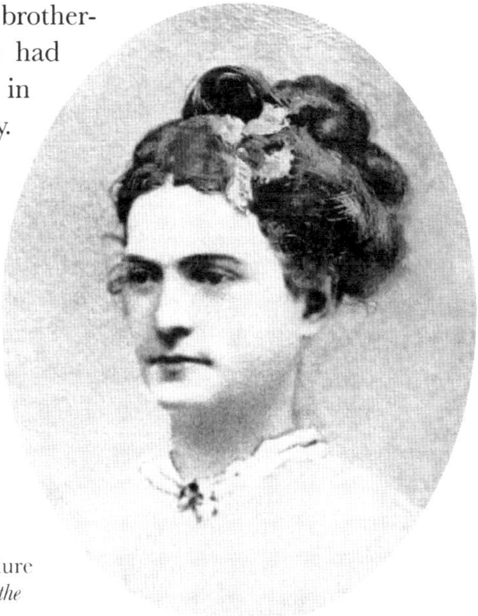

Eliza Frances Andrews, from a photo taken probably in 1860. Daughter of a Washington, Georgia judge, Andrews was an ardent Confederate while her father remained staunchly a Union man. Her wartime diary provides a colorful picture of life at home during the war. *Courtesy of the Library of Congress.*

along the Savannah River that was farmed by fifty-four slaves. A former state legislator, he was a fierce political supporter of his friend and sometimes law associate Robert A. Toombs, the brilliant and bombastic, mercurial and often intemperate, eloquent and often effusively profane former congressman and U.S. senator from Georgia, who had his home in Washington, county seat of Wilkes County, just south of Elbert County, both counties his political stronghold in northeast Georgia. Like Toombs, McIntosh had supported former U.S. vice president John C. Breckinridge as the choice of Southern Democrats in the presidential election of 1860, even being selected as one of Georgia's electors for Breckinridge. Also like Toombs, with the election of the Republican Abraham Lincoln to the presidency, he had seen no way toward a peaceful resolution to the political divisions of the North and South over slavery and states' rights and had stood firmly for secession. In that, he was typical of many of his class and position.[6]

Secession in many ways divided Georgia as much as it divided the American republic. Not in Elbert County, however, which had gone heavily for Breckinridge and the secession-leaning Southern Democrat platform in the election of 1860 and whose delegates to a state convention on the secession issue had solidly backed pulling out of the Union. When the news reached Elberton that secession had become a fact, the town broke out in celebration. Celebrants set bonfires ablaze and paraded through town by torchlight. Local political leaders gave speeches in the fire-lit square. Founded in 1803, Elberton had supplanted in the locale the declining late eighteenth-century river town of Petersburg, once the third largest town in Georgia, but still had fewer than 500 white residents, according to the 1860 census, and was at the center of a county of about 4,700 residents whose mainstay was farming, whether plantations or smaller farms. Those not listed as farmers in the census generally belonged to the trades that supplied or fed off of agriculture: merchants; blacksmiths, such as Peter J. Shannon, who marched off as a second lieutenant in the McIntosh Volunteers; other mechanics; and livestock dealers, among others. Two men listed themselves as a rock blaster and a rock cutter, perhaps presaging the town's postwar rise as a center for that industry. A total of 480 slave owners owned 5,711 slaves in the county, according to the 1860 census slave schedules, including 27 owners who, like McIntosh, owned more than 40 slaves. Lincoln's election had very early stirred Elbert County to action. Within days after the results were official, a county convention had issued a resolution declaring Lincoln's election a hazard to the Southern social order and way of life and demanding that states' rights be affirmed and calling for nullification of any federal authority contrary to states' rights within Georgia. If this could not be done within the Union, then Elbert County would support a move for Southern independence.[7]

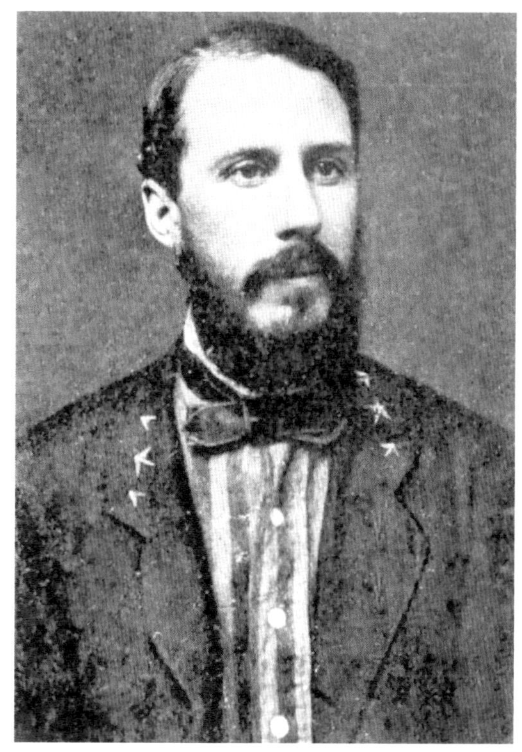

Edward Porter Alexander of Washington, Georgia. A U.S. Army lieutenant when the war broke out, he rose in the Confederate ranks to brigadier general by the war's end. Best known as a masterful artilleryman and engineer, Alexander would play a key role in trying to recover the stolen gold and silver specie of the Richmond banks. *Courtesy of the Library of Congress.*

In Washington, twenty-five miles to the south, the story was much the same. A town of about 2,200, of whom about one-third were white, the town was incorporated in 1780 and was now the county seat of Wilkes County, a wealthy planting community. By 1860, 618 slave owners in Wilkes County held 7,953 slaves, with 126 owners having more than 20. It was home to a branch of the Bank of Georgia as well as the end station for a spur rail line of the Georgia Railroad that connected Augusta and Atlanta and had the beginnings of developing industry. Washington had been at the crossroads of so much of the history and politics of the region since it had grown up around a 1770s pioneer settlement in Revolutionary times and was now turning the page to begin a new chapter. "I shall never forget that night when news came that Georgia had seceded," wrote Eliza Frances Andrews, twenty years old at the time. "...The people of the village were celebrating the event with bonfires and bell ringing and speechmaking." Young Eliza's own father, Judge Garnett Andrews, was not among them. A former judge of the northeast Georgia circuit, Garnett Andrews was a friend and longtime political ally of Robert Toombs but could not bring himself to also support Georgia's seceding. As the celebrations went on in the streets of Washington, the judge kept in his house, darkened the windows and "paced up and down the room in the greatest agitation." Every so often, Eliza Andrews chronicled, he would stop and say, "Poor fools! They may ring their bells now, but they will wring their hands—yes, and their hearts, too—before they are done with it."[8]

Garnett Andrews stood in for a great many Georgians in the lead-up to secession, as had his friend and neighbor, Congressman Alexander H. Stephens. A slave owner himself, Andrews believed Lincoln's declarations that slavery where it existed would not be interfered with, but in any case, his devotion to the Union was strong. Unlike Stephens, however, he never wavered in this commitment once secession became a fact, remaining a staunch Union man throughout the war. So highly regarded was he, however, that this caused him no real hardship during the war years, except perhaps when his offer to serve as a judge under the Confederate government was declined. Interestingly, his strong Unionist sentiments had little effect on his children. Young Eliza and her siblings were all staunch supporters of secession. And though her father had forbidden Eliza and her sister, Metta, from taking part in the celebration in the streets, he did not try to dissuade his sons, Henry and Garnett, from joining in. Neither, according to Eliza, did he try to stop his sons from joining a local company destined for the Confederate army: "I am sure he would not have wished to see them fighting against the South." In her own way, however, Eliza had her part in the celebration. She had secretly helped make the flag carried through the streets and around Washington's square by the celebrants, the "Bonnie Blue Flag" with its five-pointed white star, sewn from material her brother Henry had provided.[9]

One of Washington's native sons would not learn of Georgia's secession until about four weeks after his hometown celebrated it. In far-off Fort Steilacoom, in Washington Territory, First Lieutenant Edward Porter Alexander, U.S. Army Corps of Engineers, faced the same decision as other Southerners serving in blue uniforms, and he had made up his mind: "I knew that I would finally have to resign from the U.S. Army."

The thirty-year-old Alexander was a rising star in the army engineering corps. A son of one of Washington's oldest and most prominent families, Alexander had decided at age fourteen that he wanted to attend the U.S. Military Academy at West Point, impressed by the two graduates who had married his older sisters, future Confederate generals Alexander R. Lawton and Jeremy F. Gilmer. Family friend Robert Toombs, in time the father-in-law of Porter's brother Felix, opened the way for Alexander's appointment to the academy, and he graduated third out of thirty-eight newly minted

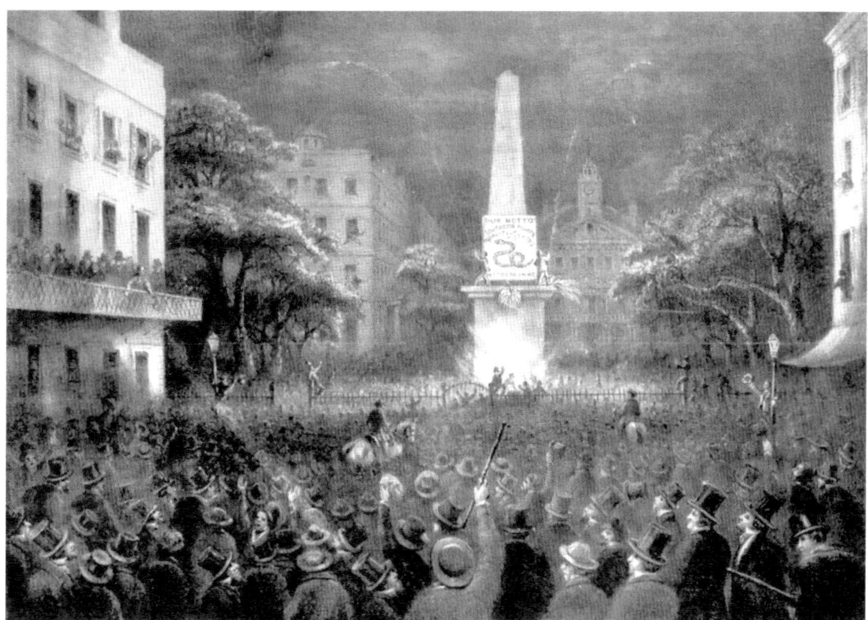

The first flag of independence raised in the South on November 8, 1860, by the citizens of Savannah, Georgia, was prompted by news of Lincoln's election. A resolution was adopted for a state secession convention. In this nocturnal scene, the square is crowded with animated spectators surrounding an obelisk, where a banner emblazoned with the image of a coiled rattlesnake and the words "Our Motto Southern Rights, Equality of the States, Don't Tread on Me" is displayed. The scene is lit by fireworks and a bonfire. The lithograph appeared in a Savannah newspaper within days and spread to other publications. *Courtesy of the Library of Congress.*

officers in the class of 1857, receiving a coveted commission as a lieutenant of engineers. Wherever he was posted, he earned the highest praises, an engineer by his very nature as well as by training. Married to a Virginia belle in April 1860, he had watched the national political cauldron bubble. "As soon as the right to secede was denied by the North, I strongly approved of its assertion and maintenance by force if necessary," Alexander recalled years later. "And being young and ambitious in my profession, I was anxious to take my part in whatever was going on."[10]

Reassigned to San Francisco in early 1861 to oversee fortification of Alcatraz Island, he resigned his commission as soon as he reached the city, asking his immediate superior to forward it and grant him leave so he would not be kept in California awaiting its acceptance. Lieutenant James B. MacPherson argued with his new young assistant to remain in the army. The Ohioan averred that the South faced a hopeless fight if war came.

The younger Alexander, he said, would likely remain stationed on the West Coast during any conflict, perhaps as ranking engineer, which opened a lot of opportunities.

"His earnest talk impressed me deeply & made me realize that a crisis in my life was at hand," Alexander reflected years later. "But I felt utterly helpless to avert it or even to debate what I should do." He could not argue against MacPherson's case, either for the South or for himself, yet still Alexander could give only one answer: "Mac, my people are going to war, & war for our liberty. If I don't come & bear my part they will believe me a coward—and I will feel that I am occupying the position of one. I must go & take my chances."[11]

Alexander was commissioned a captain of engineers in the Confederate army and by the end of 1861 was a lieutenant colonel, with engineering and ordnance his main duties. His greatest tests would come as the preeminent artillerist of the Army of Northern Virginia's First Corps, where, among other feats, he organized the bombardment of the Union army center on July 3, 1863, at Gettysburg before the final Confederate attack led by Pickett's division. He would end the war as a brigadier general. He and MacPherson would never meet again. MacPherson's star rose in the western campaigns, but he would die in Georgia, killed at the Battle of Atlanta on July 22, 1864. It was said by some present that at the news the scourge of Georgia, General William T. Sherman, wept.[12]

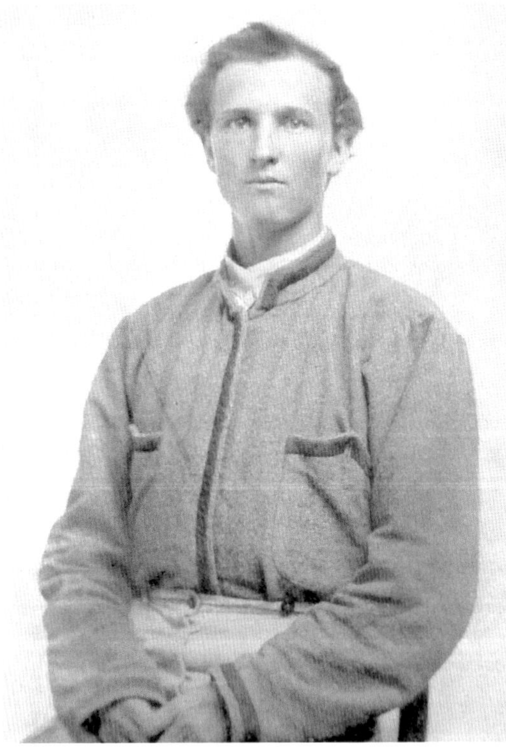

Lieutenant Horatio David, Company B, Sixteenth Georgia Infantry. Eighteen years old in 1860 and living in Jackson County, northeast of Athens, David was typical of the young Georgians who went off to war in 1861. David was paroled in Athens on May 8, 1865. *Courtesy of the Library of Congress.*

Word of Georgia's secession reached Athens on the morning of January 21, 1861, two days after the ordinance of secession was passed, and by night the city was in full celebration. Sitting on the banks of the Oconee River, in Clarke County, Athens had about 4,000 residents in 1860, split nearly half and half between white and black, with 1,955 whites, 1,890 slaves and 1 registered free black. The city was home to the University of Georgia, still called Franklin College by most after the name of its oldest building, and was the cultural, financial and industrial epicenter of northeast Georgia. It had had gas-lit streets since the early 1850s and modern fire companies supported by public cisterns. Two banks, one building and loan association and three insurance companies called the city home, and it also boasted small manufacturing industries such as foundries that employed skilled artisans. Other manufacturers included the Pioneer Paper Mill, one of the few of its kind in the South. The major industries, however, were three cotton mills, only one of which, the Athens Manufacturing Company, was actually in the city limits. These, in their size and numbers, had earned the city the early nickname the "Manchester of the South" after the British textile city. One of the first railroad lines in the state had connected Athens with Augusta in 1841. The completion of the line to Marthasville, later Atlanta, in 1845 had left Athens, like Washington, at the end of a spur. There were plans throughout the 1850s to connect Athens to towns to its north and east, setting in iron its status as the major city of the region, but Georgia's secession found the plans far from realized. Probably few gave any thought to such plans in 1860 and early 1861, as the city had been in the grip of the great debate.[13]

Athens was the political stronghold of Howell Cobb, once the powerful Speaker of the U.S. House of Representatives and now in 1860 the secretary of the treasury in the administration of President James Buchanan. On the ground in Georgia, Cobb and his influence and designs were most often represented, until his resignation from the cabinet in December 1860, by his younger brother Thomas R.R. Cobb, who had made a name for himself as a legal scholar, not least for being one of the founding professors of the University of Georgia's school of law. Howell Cobb had been a staunch Unionist ten years before when, as congressmen, he, Robert Toombs and Alexander Stephens had crafted the Georgia Platform, a compromise and statement of principle that had dampened enthusiasm for secessionist thoughts at the time, but he had sniffed the changing political winds, and so Thomas Cobb had gone forth as one of the most outspoken and persuasive voices for Southern independence.[14]

The city's first celebration had actually come on December 22, 1860, when word of South Carolina's secession two days before, the first after Lincoln's election, reached town. Fifteen cannon were fired at noon by the local militia artillery company, and a torch-lit procession wound through the town that evening, celebrants carrying a flag with one large star representing South Carolina surrounded by fourteen smaller stars and the inscription "Protect Our Homes." Outside Thomas Cobb's stately mansion hung a banner that read "Resistance to Abolition Is Obedience to God."[15]

Despite the Cobbs and the evident joy by many that night at the idea of disunion, that had not always been the prevailing wind blowing through Athens. The election of 1860—with Southern Democrat John C. Breckinridge, Northern Democrat Stephen Douglas and the Constitutional Party's John Bell vying for Georgians' votes—had been hard fought in debate and in the newspaper editorials of both the pro-Cobb *Athens Banner* and the more conservative Whig relic *Southern Watchman*, edited by the unsparing John H. Christy. In August, Howell Cobb made a speech in Athens in favor of Breckinridge, hailed as one of his best orations ever given. Also in August, the *Watchman* had championed the formation in Athens of the Constitutional Union Club, at which one of the most frequent and outspoken speakers in favor of seeking redress of Southern grievances within the Union was Amos T. Akerman, of Elberton. Akerman, a New Hampshire transplant, was a prominent attorney in Elberton and also owned acreage and slaves in Elbert County. He was also, as we will see, a man with a curious destiny, considering his time and place. When the Athens city votes were tallied in November, in perhaps a true gauge of the Cobbs' influence on their home ground, the Unionist Bell had 383 votes to Breckinridge's 334, with Douglas far behind at 40. In the county as a whole, Bell's margin was wider, with 695 votes to Breckinridge's 451 and Douglas finishing with only 57. Breckinridge finished first in Georgia's polling overall, though he lacked a clear majority. So like some other places in Georgia, Athens and its vicinity did not favor a rush to Southern independence. But also as in other places in Georgia, when the votes were finally counted in the national election, a change set in. Not all who favored feared a rush to disunion, but enough.[16]

One of the first happenings in Athens after the election was a meeting on November 10 to beef up the police force. Until then, it had consisted of a town marshal, an assistant marshal and up to six officers who patrolled the city at night. Fears of slave insurrections had been building throughout the South for over a year, since abolitionist John Brown had attempted to foment one in Virginia. That Lincoln's election would further stoke the danger had been a common theme throughout the presidential campaign in the South. Now the fact of his election was pounded home by the secessionists as virtually guaranteeing that the haunting fear of general insurrection would become reality, with Thomas Cobb one of the loudest sirens. Thomas Cobb, in fact, was appointed to the committee that eventually recommended expanding the city police force as much as possible, to form auxiliary volunteer police forces in each district, to urge more forceful patrolling out in the county and to urge plantation owners to keep a closer watch on their laboring property. A special committee was also appointed to investigate allegations of plotted slave insurrections.[17]

At about the same time, five days after the election, a lifelong resident of Clarke County was overheard speaking in favor of free-soil, the idea that slavery could be prohibited in a place by law. He was "arrested" and taken to the city hall for trial before an informal tribunal, where the man denied any wrongdoing. Thomas Cobb, summoned to the drumhead proceeding, spoke for the defense, asking that the man, never named in any account, be released with the warning that any future like offense should bring a hanging. The *Watchman*'s John Christy editorialized that dissenters should keep their opinions to themselves lest they court lynch mobs. Christy's own commitment to the Union, in fact, seemed to waver in the days after the election, with an editorial among the first to call for a state convention to gauge the voters' sentiment. Then perhaps, wrote Christy, the fifteen slave states should call a convention for unity, with an aim of negotiating to ensure states' rights or to secede together.[18]

Still, hope for the Union continued in the drawing rooms of Athens even if dissent was quashed on the streets. On the same night that many in Athens celebrated South Carolina's secession, Athenians opposed to Georgia's rushing to follow suit met in the then Clarke County seat at Watkinsville, the meeting presided over by William McIntosh's brother-in-law, Judge Young L.G. Harris, and editor Christy. The group affirmed a desire to redress Southern grievances from within the Union, with secession a last resort. They also selected three delegates to the state convention that had been called on the secession question. The delegates were sworn to act only as they thought best. A week earlier, the Cobb faction had also held a meeting and elected three delegates, including Thomas Cobb himself. One man, Asbury Hull, was selected as a delegate by both groups. When the votes were counted after the January 2, 1861 polling for the county's delegates to the state convention, the three secessionist delegates, including Cobb and Hull, were selected overwhelmingly. In the *Watchman*, Christy warned of civil war—"Fraternal blood will shed in profusion within the next sixty days"—and evinced little belief that political leaders could or would avert calamity. "If they possessed any genuine patriotism, settlement, honorable and satisfactory to all, might be effected in a short time. But we have well nigh lost all hope."[19]

The night that secession was a known fact in Athens, the local militia artillery, the Troup Artillery, fired a one-hundred-gun salute, and another torch-lit procession, led off this time by university students, wound through the streets. The crowd burned an effigy of General Winfield Scott. The Virginia-born Scott, general in chief of the United States Army, had been loud and impolitic in his condemnation of secession as essentially treasonous, so in the seceding South, he was seen as a traitor himself. A balloon inscribed with the names of all the seceding states so far was set adrift on the night air. The balloon, the editor of the pro-secession *Athens Banner* waxed eloquent, "sailed toward the South-West—where the star of Southern Empire must take its way—tremendous cheers greeted the good omen."[20]

Over the next few weeks, military companies besides those already making up the local militia formed and drilled. One company, the Lumpkin Law School Cadets, formed and agreed to suspend their legal studies "for the purpose of drilling and mutually instructing ourselves in military tactics and the science of war." The Troup Artillery was the first to leave Athens, on April 24, bound for the coastal defenses near Savannah. Their departure was "the grandest civic and military display Athens has ever witnessed," according to one observer. The unit marched to the railroad depot led by a band and accompanied by the other marching units such as the Oconee Cavalry and the Athens Guards, the fire department and a crowd estimated at between two thousand and five thousand. The artillerymen had, as the *Athens Banner*'s editorial framed it, "nobly responded to their country's call, to drive back from her soil those who would pollute it with their steps." Other observers were less highflying in their rhetoric and struck more at the essence of the scene. "Today Athens sent a company to the wars," wrote George D. Smith, a newly elected lieutenant in the Lumpkin Law School Cadets. "The town is in a great state of excitement, everybody wants to go fight."

The other units would leave in a matter of days, but to less grandiose sendoffs. William Sammons Grady, merchant, sawmill owner and half owner of a plant that made gas from pine wood, marched off at the head of a company he had formed. A Union man, Grady nevertheless threw in with the Confederacy once Georgia seceded. He would become a captain in the Twenty-fifth North Carolina Regiment. As he went to war, he left

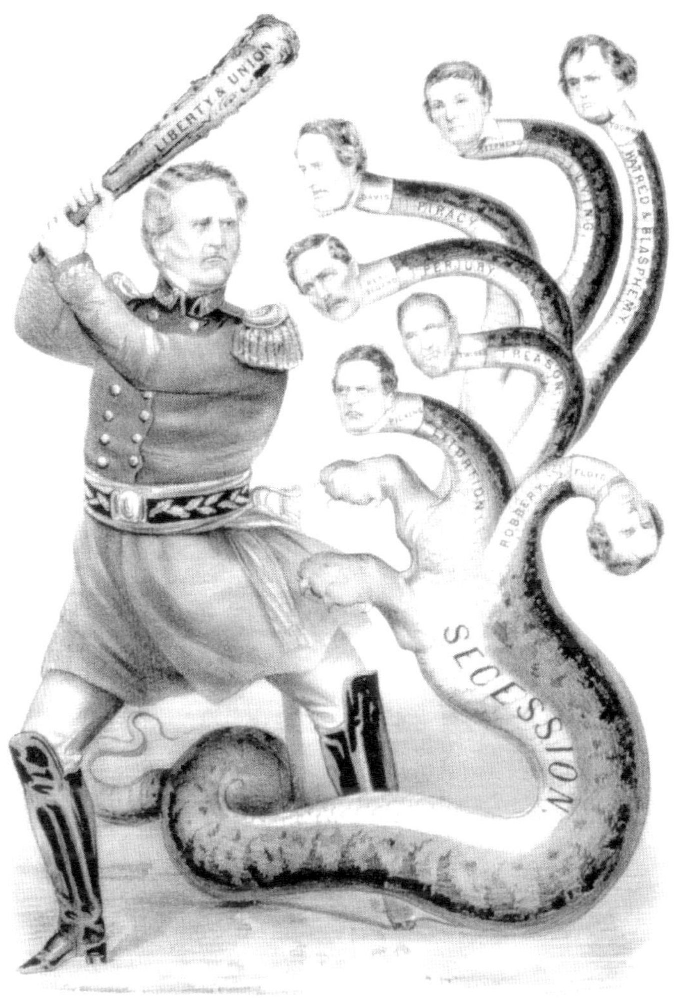

THE HERCULES OF THE UNION,

A Currier & Ives lithograph that appeared in 1861 as a tribute to commander of Union forces General Winfield Scott, shown as the mythical Hercules slaying the many-headed dragon or hydra, symbolizing the secession of the Confederate states. Scott, wielding a great club "Liberty and Union," is about to strike the beast. The hydra has seven heads, each representing a prominent Southern leader. The neck of each Southerner depicted is labeled with a vice or crime associated with him. Robert Toombs (Hatred and Blasphemy) and Alexander Stephens (Lying) occupy prominent places near the top, along with Jefferson Davis (Piracy). Like other editorializing depictions, it expressed a popular sentiment in the North while fanning the flames of conflict. *Courtesy of the Library of Congress.*

behind his family, which included his oldest son, ten-year-old Henry Woodfin Grady.[21]

Not every town and village met the news of secession with celebration. In Pickens County, on the northwestern fringe of what was considered northeast Georgia, a strong group of Unionists kept the United States flag flying at the county courthouse weeks after the news of Georgia's secession came. In Dahlonega, in Lumpkin County, a group threatened to seize the branch of the U.S. Mint there and hold it for the Union. This prompted another group to form as a guard for the mint, preserving it for the forming Confederacy.

The history of these mountainous northern counties at the fringe of northeast Georgia differed from that of the piedmont along the upper middle Savannah Valley westward to Athens. It had been the territory of the Cherokee in living memory, with a major gold rush in the late 1820s near what became Dahlonega loosening the Cherokees' hold on the land, which became complete with the tribe's removal west of the Mississippi in the 1830s. The region's recent frontier past had left its stamp. Slavery was less a vital part of the economy of smaller farms, timber and gristmills, operated by their owners and their families with few or no slaves. In Lumpkin County, centered on Dahlonega, a city fit to rival Athens, slaves made up only 10 percent of the population, compared to the 50 percent or more common in the plantation belt. And free blacks, while a clear minority, were more often seen. One of Lumpkin County's most successful businessmen in 1860, in fact, was James "Free Jim" Bosclair, owner of a dry goods store, a saloon and an icehouse. All these stemmed, purportedly, from a gold find Bosclair had made in the 1830s gold rush, apparently enough to gain both his freedom and a grubstake. Like all free blacks, Bosclair was required to have a white man stand for all business dealings of his enterprises, but there was no question as to the real ownership. All these counties would see some measure of continuing strife over secession throughout the war, even raiding parties of Unionist guerrillas bent on murder and plunder. But Georgia counties farther north and to the northwest would see far more by comparison. The mountain counties would also send men to the Confederate army, with sendoffs just as bubbling with enthusiasm. The last week of June 1861, the Blue Ridge Rifles, one of Lumpkin's first companies, marched through the streets of Dahlonega. A Methodist preacher called down the blessings of heaven on the men, and each man was presented with a Bible.[22]

Some chose service in state forces, believing the duty would be easier, certainly closer to home and, probably, safer. E.H. Sutton, of near the Batesville community of Habersham County, enlisted in the Georgia State troops in the

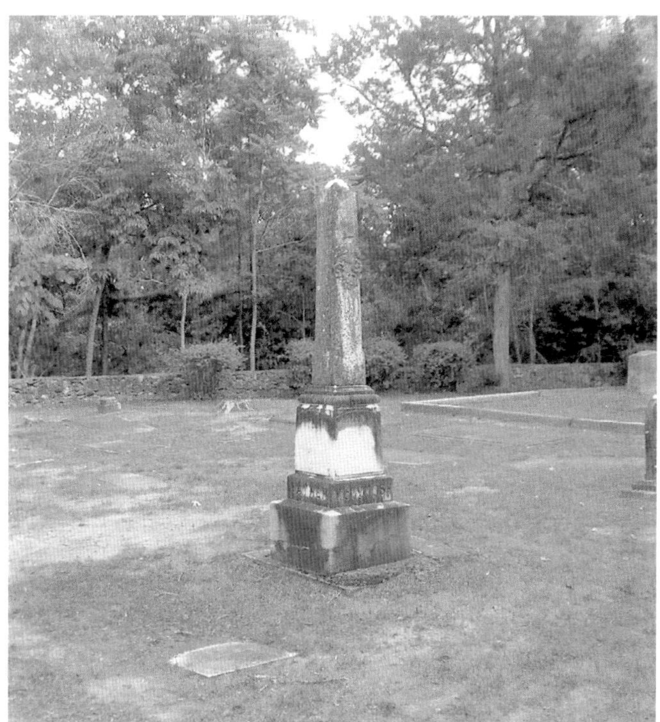

This page: These stones mark the grave of Colonel William M. McIntosh in the Heard Cemetery, in Heardmont, Elbert County. After his death in Richmond in June 1862, his wife and his manservant brought his body back to Elbert County.

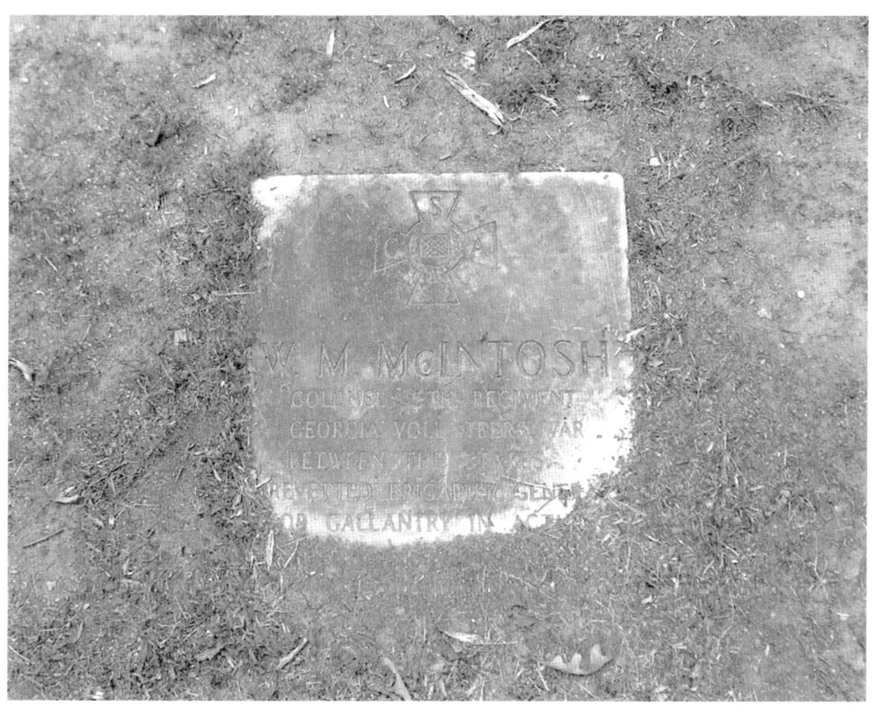

fall of 1861 after a call out by Georgia governor Joseph Brown, who feared an attack on the state's coasts. "I felt sure I would have to go sooner or later and take my turn at service somewhere," Sutton related in his memoir forty-six years later. "So I decided to go into State service for six months supposing that would clear me of being forced into service again." Sutton's uncle carried him and eight others by wagon to Dahlonega, where the young farm boy volunteers were fêted in style. "We were given all we could eat and drink and a good bed to sleep in," Sutton recalled, and the men were also roundly entertained by the people of Dahlonega. From there, the group traveled northwest to Carterville, where they became members of the Eighth Georgia State Troops. They elected officers and heard many speeches from the winners, most predicting the war would be over quickly, within three months, "just a breakfast spell." Sutton's cousin W.L. Sutton, called on to speak, disagreed: "These Yankees will fight, and if we whip them it will have to be by hard fighting." Cousin E.H. recalled being ashamed of the speech at the time. He also remembered revisiting his cousin's words over the following years.[23]

The Eighth Georgia State Troops were sent to Camp Harrison, below Savannah, the trip from Cartersville to Atlanta occasioning the first train ride for many of the young men. Crowds stood along the rails near villages and towns, waving and cheering. At stops, the men were fed like kings. It was a slice of heaven before the hell, because once the men were in the coastal camp, meningitis—"brain fever," as the novice soldiers called it—which Sutton attributed to the brackish water from shallow coastal wells, would decimate the regiment. Sutton himself barely survived. The experience of camp life and its often companion, disease (the regiment had already suffered an outbreak of measles in Cartersville), did not quell any rising of a patriotic ardor or an age-old desire that young Singleton McIntosh knew, to see the apparent excitement of war.

In May 1862, Governor Brown visited the camp and asked the regiment to volunteer for another six months' service. Troops from the mountains would be stationed near their homes, Brown promised, but most of all, he said, he would keep them in the state and out of the clutches of the Conscription Act, passed by the Confederate Congress the month before. Throughout the rest of the war, the Confederate government's conscription of Georgians into the Confederate States Army would be one of Brown's two main bones of contention with Jefferson Davis's government. (The other bone would be Confederate taxation.) It would alienate the state, Brown's government and Brown himself from the Confederate national government and threaten the sometimes tenuous union of the seceded states.[24]

Sutton and his cohorts refused the governor, however, eager now to see the fighting. "Most of us wished to go to the front," Sutton recalled, "and to get part of the glory awarded to our country's brave defenders." After a furlough home, Sutton and his friends volunteered for Company C of the Twenty-fourth Georgia Infantry, which included companies from Franklin, Hart and Hall Counties, among others. On July 13, 1862, they started for Virginia to join the regiment. (Sutton would serve under the Cobb brothers and would be on hand on December 13 of that year at Fredericksburg to see Thomas Cobb carried off the field with his mortal wound.)[25]

Over that June and July of 1862, the war took a critical turn. The Confederate Army of Northern Virginia, now under the command of General Robert E. Lee, had driven the Union Army of the Potomac from the York-James peninsula, and Lee was now thinking of turning northward to face another Union army cobbled together to attack toward the Confederate capital from a different direction. The result would be perhaps Lee's most complete strategic and tactical victory at the Battle of Second Manassas in late August. Confederate fortunes, at low ebb at the time that Colonel William McIntosh had sat in his tent writing his son on the travails of soldiering, were now offering chances of victory that Lee was taking at the flood.

McIntosh had heard the tolling of the changing fortunes, in a way. The artillery fire he noted hearing in the letter to his son Singleton was very likely the opening of what became known as the Battle of Seven Pines. The battle was indecisive from almost every angle but one. The Confederate commanding general, Joseph E. Johnston, was wounded. President Jefferson Davis handed command of the army to the nearest available man he trusted, Lee, his chief military advisor. It would prove to be one of the most profound decisions of the war.

Colonel McIntosh would never know that, however. On June 27, during a skirmishing action at a place called Garnett's Farm during Lee's Seven Days Battles that drove the Army of the Potomac from the York-James peninsula, a Federal bullet tore through his chest.

Robert Toombs, by this time resigned from his position as Confederate secretary of state and a brigadier general, commanded the brigade that included the Fifteenth Georgia. Ordered to send skirmishers forward, he had ordered in the Second and Fifteenth Georgia and cried openly as McIntosh was taken from the field. The Fifteenth Georgia's surgeon asked him why. He responded, "I have been forced, by order of that damned [General John Bankhead] Magruder, to send McIntosh, one of the best men God ever made, to his certain death."[26]

Toombs proved prophetic. McIntosh died in a Richmond hospital three days later, but he would be promoted posthumously to brigadier general for his gallantry.

That fall, Singleton McIntosh, still a few months shy of his eighteenth birthday, left the Georgia Military Institute and joined the Seventh Georgia Cavalry.[27]

Chapter 2

"...The Crisis We Are in the Midst Of..."

Rain fell hard virtually all over Georgia on Wednesday, January 2, 1861, and that was a cause of both hope and despair to some Georgians, depending on which side of the secession question they fell.

In his home in Crawfordville, about twenty miles from Washington, Alexander Hamilton Stephens, an ardent opponent of Georgia seceding, described it as "the worst day for an election I ever saw in Georgia."

When the sickly Stephens agreed to venture out and speak at the Taliaferro County courthouse in Crawfordville, he found about one hundred men gathered after having voted, some inside, some on the portico, but "all dripping with wet."

From Sparta, in Hancock County, about thirty miles farther south in middle Georgia, Stephens's half brother Linton Stephens wrote him that the rain had made the turnout of the voters thin. The younger Stephens found some hope in this, however. "The secessionists are disappointed here," he wrote, adding that the rain might have had a similar effect across the state.

Alexander, though, was pessimistic. The rain, he said, "told greatly against the Conservative cause...It really appears as if Providence were on the other side."[28]

What counted most, in the end, was that Georgia's governor, Joseph Brown, was on the side of the secessionist cause.

The voters on January 2 were not deciding the issue directly. They were choosing delegates to a state convention on the secession question. Even now, historians can't agree on a final tally from all the various local voting. One

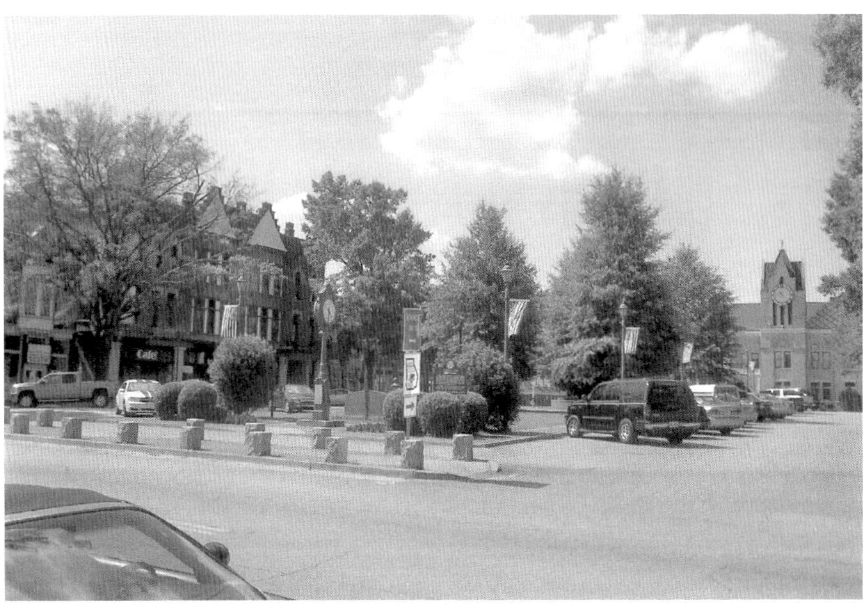

Washington's square in 2014. In the spring of 1865, paroled Confederate soldiers thronged this square as Washington became a way station for men heading home from war. *Author's photograph.*

study estimates the true result at 44,152 to 41,632, in favor of secession, barely more than 51 percent. Another study estimates the tally at 42,744 to 41,717 in favor of those opposed to immediate secession, barely more than 50 percent. Whatever the truth, the estimates show the opinion of the voting public almost evenly divided on the most acute political crisis most had ever seen.[29]

An official result of the January vote, however, was never made public. A resolution raised at the later state convention to require the governor to publish the results was voted down. It wasn't until April, when Georgia was solidly in the Confederacy, that Brown released a state tally, and only then after an inquiry by Georgians too prominent to ignore. He reported a margin of victory for secessionist of over 13,000, the numbers 50,243 votes for secessionist delegates to 37,123 votes for the opposition. The numbers of votes for secession are almost certainly exaggerated, and the very fact that the results were still being questioned hard so long after the fact strongly suggests that opinion was hardly so lopsided.[30]

The battle over whether to secede broke down to divisions in class and geography and to long-simmering fears and the raw politics that exploited them, all with a cast of characters as gargantuan in their egos and ambitions as they appeared larger than life to many even in their own day—even if they were like Alexander Stephens, frail, sickly and probably never in his life weighing over one hundred pounds.

Where a Georgian stood on secession in late 1860 could be gauged at least in part by what he saw from his front door.

For the better part of over two generations, two national issues had defined the political differences between the northern and southern states: the protective tariffs supported by northern manufacturing interests—and just as vigorously opposed by the southern planters—and slavery and its potential spread westward. It was a tariff passed in 1828 that had brought the first major crisis in 1832–33, the so-called Nullification Crisis. The state of South Carolina, driven by its fiery states' rights champion, then vice president John C. Calhoun, decided to nullify collection of the tariff at its ports. President Andrew Jackson met the crisis with a fierce and determined assertion of federal powers, and in the end, South Carolina backed down. Before that, however, talk of secession arose, seriously, for the first time, by Calhoun in his *South Carolina Exposition and Protest*. Secession was hardly a new idea in the young American republic and hardly one confined to the South. New Englanders had raised the prospect as far back as the War of 1812, which many in that region had opposed. But with Calhoun's pronouncement, it became a wild card in the political game the North and South would play for nearly the next thirty years.[31]

The tariff issue simmered following the Nullification Crisis, and some tariffs were actually reduced. The late 1840s and early 1850s saw vibrant economic growth, but the Panic of 1857, spurred by bank failures, resurrected the idea of high protective tariffs in earnest. The South had reason to fear. Cotton exports to Europe, after the northern textile mills and the sprouting southern ones had been fed, were 70 percent of the United States' exports by 1860. Most of the cotton did not sail directly from southern ports but was channeled through northern ports. But any tariff on predominantly European manufactured goods, coming mainly from Great Britain and France, would impact the importing agricultural South, not just in prices paid for manufactured articles but also in lower cotton prices. One way or another, southern representatives argued, the South would suffer a burden from the tariff. Not the least of this burden would be the southern states paying a disproportionate share of federal revenues, almost solely derived from excise taxes on imports, while the North benefited from federal internal improvements and other federal expenditures in far greater proportion than the South.[32]

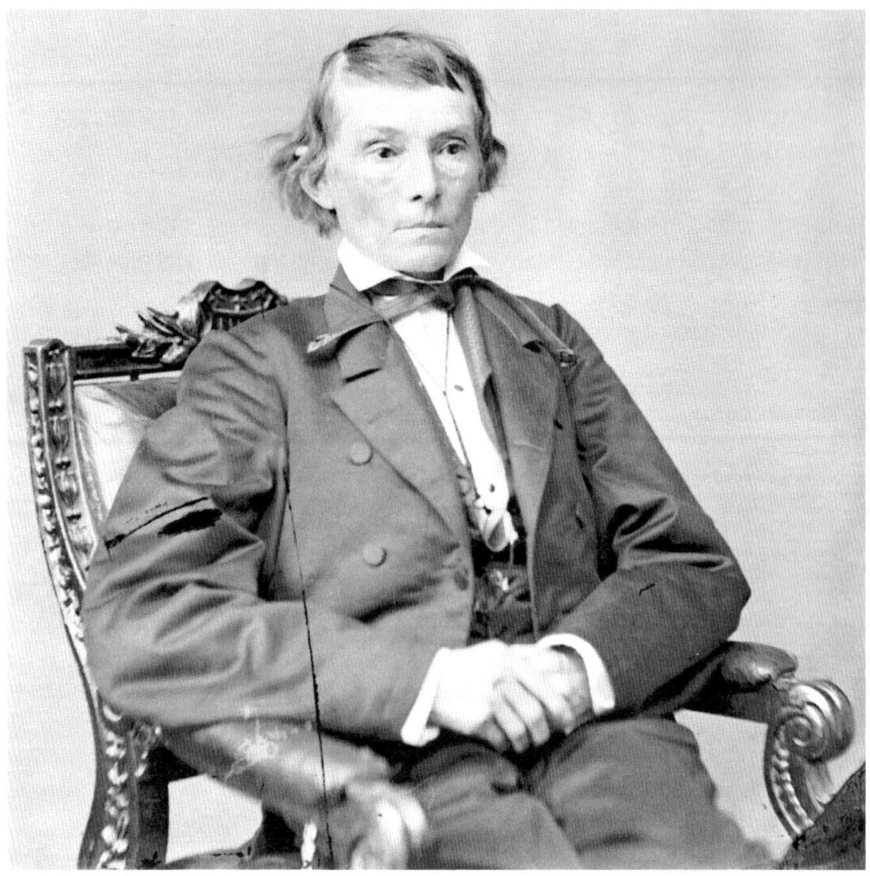

Alexander H. Stephens, from a wartime photograph. The lifelong best friend of Robert Toombs, Stephens nevertheless bitterly opposed his old compatriot over secession. But Stephens was an arch supporter of Southern rights, and when secession became a fact, he became vice-president of the Confederacy, though often at odds with Jefferson Davis. *Courtesy of the Library of Congress.*

What became known as the Morrill Tariff, named for the Vermont congressman who principally drafted it, supported by Abraham Lincoln and the Republican Party and raising duties to an average of 36 percent on imported manufactured articles, was an issue in the election of 1860. Both Stephen Douglas, the Northern Democratic candidate, and John C. Breckinridge, the Southern Democratic candidate, opposed it. Southern representatives stalled the advance of the tariff in the 1859 and 1860 sessions of Congress, but Republicans looked forward to a renewed push after the new national elections. Ironically, the bill would pass by a comfortable margin on March 2, 1861, over two weeks before Lincoln's inauguration, aided by the congressional delegations of the already seceded Southern states being absent.[33]

IN THE RENEWED FLARE-UP of secessionist talk stemming from the prospect of Lincoln's election and then the fact of it, the tariff issue, very real and very portentous in its potential effects on the South, would be heard but only as a murmur amid the shouts that slavery faced its gravest threat. A tariff, after all, however real its effects, is a nebulous thing. Slavery a Southerner saw everywhere and all around him, often inside his home but certainly the moment he set foot through his front door.

As twentieth-century analysis of the voting patterns in the January 2, 1860 election showed, if a Georgian standing in his front door saw several hundred acres of his land tilled by dozens of his slaves, he was more likely to support seceding, especially if his nearest neighbors were planters such as himself. That made it all the more likely that what he saw was the rolling piedmont of the Savannah River Valley and the Georgia midlands that had been the final stops for the settlers of that part of Georgia who had pushed up the valley from the coast or migrated from Virginia and the upper Carolinas beginning in the 1770s. This Georgian's roots were deep and long in the gray-black and red soil, and his family was a long way from the simple stock that had first looked to the Georgia uplands as a new chance.[34]

A key, an indispensable part of this way of life, was slavery and the holding of slaves. But that simple distinction did not and could not tell the whole story. More than a few large slaveholders—such as Stephens, perhaps Georgia's most influential member of Congress—opposed secession in the beginning, believing strongly, even passionately, in the Union and the government of the U.S. Constitution, but they embraced the cause of Southern independence once secession became a fact. Others remained staunch Unionists, like Garnett Andrews. Slaveholders were a minority in the state, however, with only 37 percent of the property owners including slaves among their holdings.[35]

If a Georgian saw from his front door city streets and the walls of a factory, evidence of the tide of industrialization that had been rising in Georgia for nearly twenty years, then he also likely supported secession. The economic calamity called the Panic of 1837 had dried up capital and credit nationwide, and Georgia, largely agricultural, felt the full brunt of this until well into the 1840s, with many planters and merchants going bankrupt. The survivors pushed for a more diversified economy, for more manufacturing,

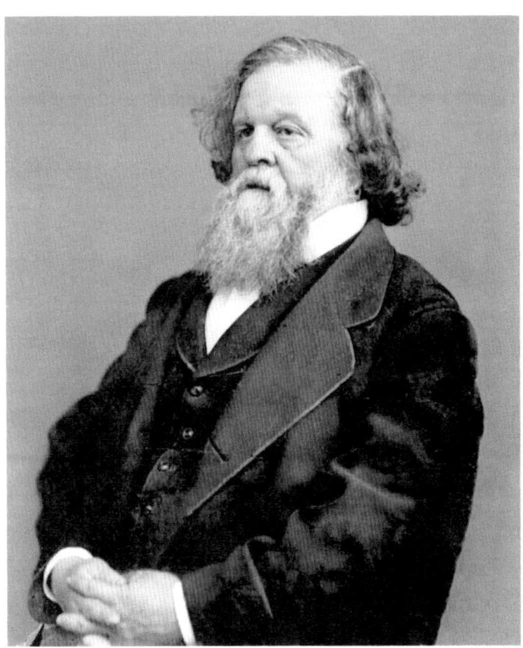

Howell Cobb, from a probable wartime photograph. A former Speaker of the U.S. House of Representatives, former governor of Georgia and former secretary of the treasury, Cobb was one of the most masterful politicians of his age. He pushed hard for secession and intrigued for a high position in the Confederate government. He failed at the latter and served most of the war in a variety of military positions for which he was ill suited. *Courtesy of the Library of Congress.*

for more banking and credit resources of their own, for more development of the state's natural resources and, to tie it all together, for more railroads. In some cases, that meant picking up railroad projects that had been abandoned during the panic. By 1860, Georgia was second, behind Virginia, among those states that seceded in its miles of railroad, with 1,404 miles, over double the 643 miles of 1850. More were planned at the time Georgia struck for disunion, such as a line linking Atlanta with Hall County, going to Hart County and eventually crossing into South Carolina. The war brought these endeavors to a halt, however. Major cities such as Augusta, Columbus and Atlanta—a city that was virtually a product of its railroad nexus—were centers of manufacturing. The state was home of 1,890 manufacturers of various sizes, including 33 textile mills. The largest single industry, based on the wholesale value of the finished products, however, was grain milling, with 378 active mills. These cosmopolitan areas, in counties where anywhere from 30 percent to 100 percent of the population were town dwellers, would vote in a range from 64 percent to 77 percent for secession.[36]

If a Georgian had leaned toward the old Whig Party when it was a power, then he likely voted for the Southern Democratic candidate, sitting Vice President John C. Breckinridge, in the election of 1860 and also, when the Georgian had to decide, leaned toward seceding. Eighty-one counties that voted at least 50 percent for Breckinridge would later vote in favor of secession in percentages ranging from 54 percent to 64 percent. Those who had hewed to the Democratic Party in the 1850s, who had likely voted for the Northern Democratic candidate Stephen A. Douglas and his vice presidential choice, former Georgia governor Herschel V. Johnson, tended to oppose seceding. Supporters of the Constitutional Party candidate, John Bell, probably most strongly opposed seceding except as a last resort—the sentiment echoed by most Breckinridge supporters, including Breckinridge-leaning newspaper editorial pages, but for the most part cast aside as soon as Lincoln's election brought home their worst fears.[37]

Breaking up the Union was a threat used by southern leaders for nearly two generations in defense of states' rights and slavery, most recently before the war during the crisis over the Compromise of 1850. Fever for secession had grown especially hot since among the political class in Alabama, Mississippi, South Carolina and Georgia, where many state leaders saw the compromise offering less protection to southern interests than touted. On that occasion, Robert Toombs and Alexander Stephens, both at the time Whig congressmen, joined with the Democrat Howell Cobb, then the powerful Speaker of the U.S. House of Representatives, to cool the fever in Georgia, stumping the state, making their case to any crowd that would gather—and all his life Toombs could draw a crowd—before an election of delegates to a called state convention to consider Georgia's response to the

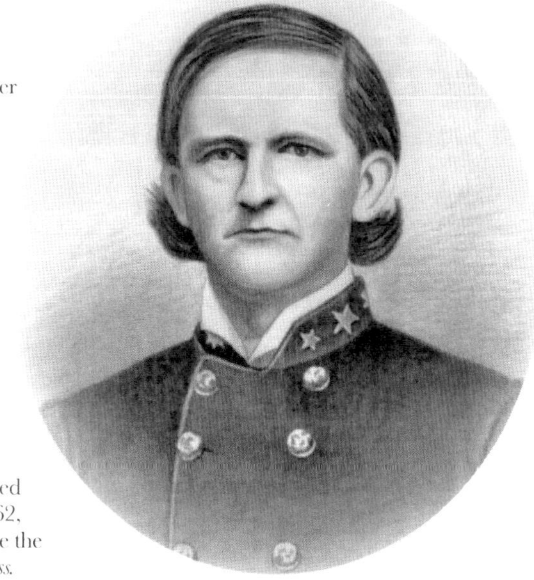

Thomas R.R. Cobb, younger brother of Howell Cobb, as well as his brother's foremost political crony. A fine legal mind, Thomas Cobb was, along with Toombs, one of the loudest voices for secession. He and his brother intrigued for high office during the Confederate government's formation but failed. He was, however, an architect of the Confederate constitution. The Army of Northern Virginia brigade he commanded held the famous stone wall on the heights above Fredericksburg against repeated Union attacks on December 13, 1862, but Thomas Cobb would not survive the battle. *Courtesy of the Library of Congress.*

Compromise. Stephens later estimated that he himself had traveled no fewer than three thousand miles back and forth across the state. In the end, the votes for Unionist delegates to Georgia's convention swamped opponents by 46,616 votes to 24,499.[38]

Out of that convention came the Georgia Platform, essentially crafted by the three. The platform affirmed a belief in the sanctity and perpetual nature of the Union, but a Union "secondary in importance only to the rights and principles it was designed to perpetuate…that will bind us to it so long as it continues to be the safeguard of those rights and principles." Critical to that, in the platform's language, was the upholding of the Fugitive Slave Bill, which some northern states refused to honor. Mississippi and Alabama ultimately adopted the platform, and the underlying principles largely shaped southern politics for most of the next decade. In Georgia politics, the struggle also set the stage for the next decade of struggle in statewide offices between hardcore southern rights advocates and those who desired to work to protect southerners' rights within the Union. The craftsmen, who also formed the Constitutional Union Party, which endured until the war, also reaped rewards. The diminutive and sickly Stephens's stature and power grew in the U.S. House of Representatives. The leonine Toombs gained greater influence over the state's national politics when he was appointed a U.S. senator from Georgia in 1851, and Howell Cobb, temporarily abandoning Washington, D.C., was elected governor. Cobb would return to national politics in March 1857 as secretary of the treasury in the Buchanan administration.[39]

The fight in Georgia over secession in late 1860 echoed this earlier fight. The Breckinridge campaign essentially adopted the principles of the Georgia Platform, holding to the Union as long as Southerners' interests were protected to the fullest. Breckinridge's finishing first of the three candidates in the state, but lacking a majority, is perhaps the most telling gauge of Georgians' sentiments at the time. But secession as a clear and determined course should Lincoln be elected was an undercurrent theme of the Breckinridge campaign even if his most outspoken supporters didn't necessarily give it voice. With Lincoln's election, however, and the apparent ascent of radical abolitionism as a more powerful force than ever—despite Lincoln's own assertions that slavery would not be interfered with where it existed—the voices for secession began to rise, playing on some of Georgians', and other Southerners', worst fears.[40]

In 1850, after all, no one had heard of John Brown. In 1860, Brown peered out of the woodcut images in southern broadsheets as the wild-eyed and biblically bearded prophet of murderous doom for all who doubted the wisdom and morality of abolishing slavery. His 1859 attempt to raise an armed slave revolt in Virginia galvanized the South's worst fears concerning the abolitionists' methods and motives. That was aided by both real and rumored acts of what appeared to be sprouts of insurrection among slaves emboldened by the events in far-off Virginia. The stories spread across the South by print and word of mouth, sometimes no doubt growing more sensational in the telling, but at their core were real events, and Georgia had its own share.[11]

A wave of fires struck across the state, attributed to slaves. A planter in Jasper County was reported to have shot and killed a slave caught setting fire to a gin house. Other incidents from near Forsyth reported slaves caught firing stored cotton. In November 1859, an Elbert County newspaper reported an outbreak of suspicious fires in the county.[12]

The result of the increased fear was that along with a stepping up of the routine patrols by forces organized by the planters came a tightening of regulations until then sometimes only loosely enforced. One such was the laws against giving or selling alcohol to slaves. It had long been the law, winked at in the rural areas, that slaves could not carry firearms. Now enforcement of the law was made strict. In the cities, including Athens, city officials took steps to discourage or end the practice of whites hiring out their slaves, who then lived not under the owners' immediate watch. This was a violation of an 1831 state law that until the crisis was often ignored. Athens discouraged the practice by imposing a 25 percent tax on the wages earned.[13]

Free blacks also came under increased scrutiny as presumed agents of abolitionists (as, indeed, some were). A litany of local ordinances was either enacted or enforced after enforcement had long been allowed to lay idle. In Alexander Stephens's Crawfordville, free blacks were barred from living on lots separate from the white guardian the law had long required them to have. They were also barred from running any form of restaurant or saloon and from dealing in livestock or farm products. Violators faced fines of up to $200 and, if unable to pay, could be sold into slavery for a time considered equivalent to the fine. In December 1859, the Georgia legislature took up the issue, closing gaps in the manumission laws that basically blocked the freeing of slaves. Other provisions barred free blacks from other states from Georgia, with selling into slavery the penalty facing violators, and tightened the laws on vagrancy as applied to the freedmen. Vagrancy became a catchall, defined as "wandering or strolling about, leading an idle, immoral or profligate course of life." Two years of slavery awaited a first offender. For a second offense, it would be life.[14]

The tension and fear mounted into 1860, with the national election looming. More acts of apparent insurrection, real and rumored, caused ripples of excitement across the state and the rest of the South, like pebbles dropped into a pool. More bloodshed fueled the fears. One such incident happened in June, when William Smith, a planter in Oglethorpe County, adjoining Elbert and Wilkes Counties, died after he was stabbed sixteen times by a slave who had refused to work when told. The slave ran but was captured the next day and taken to the county seat at Lexington. Within a day or two, the slave was taken out by a committee of locals and burned at the stake, becoming one of several instances in Georgia and across the South where the death penalty for slaves apparently in insurrection was carried out by fire.[15]

The fears were real, as were the reported acts that fueled them. Many, if not most, of the rumors of insurrectionist acts were well grounded to some degree. But for most Southerners not of the planter class, the simple fact of Lincoln's election did make their supporting secession a given. In Stephens's Crawfordville, a public meeting issued the resolve that "we do not consider the election of Lincoln and [Hannibal] Hamlin as sufficient cause for Disunion or Secession." Similar meetings in other counties saw the same decided sentiment. But here and there, in the counties with high percentages of slaves among the population, were sparks that proponents of secession could fan. Georgia's governor, Joseph E. Brown, as diehard a secessionist as ever there was, wasn't slow to act.[16]

Joseph Emerson Brown was born in the old Pickens District (now Oconee and Pickens Counties) of upstate South Carolina in 1821 but grew up in the mountains of northern Georgia. Well educated in his youth, he had taught school for a short time while he read law and later, in 1845, attended Yale Law School for a year, thanks to a benefactor. Having established his practice in Canton, Georgia, he took the natural step into politics, winning a seat in the state senate in 1849 as a fierce advocate of southern rights. In the state senate, he made a valuable friend in Linton Stephens, a relationship that later paid handsome dividends in his quest for the governor's chair. In 1855, he was elected to a judgeship in the state superior court. In 1857, he secured the Democratic nomination for governor with the help of the Stephens brothers (Linton, in fact, nominated him at the state convention), which brought with it at least nominal support from Toombs. Brown's nomination occurred in direct opposition to the desires of Howell Cobb, who supported an Athens crony, John H.

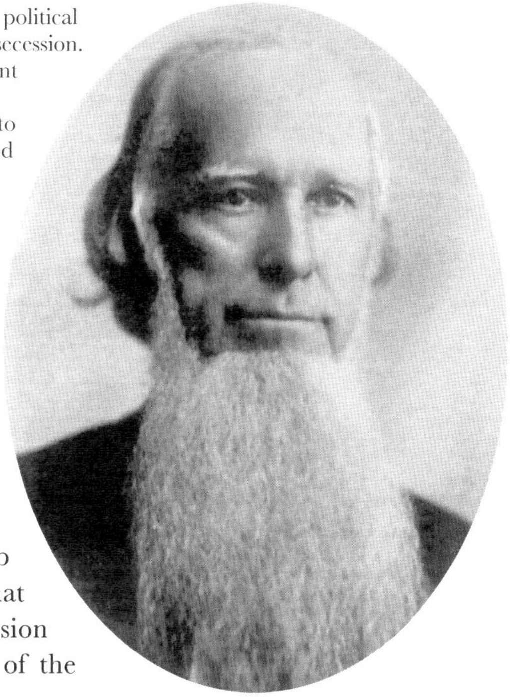

Governor Joseph E. Brown. A superb political opportunist, Brown led Georgia into secession. But he became one of the most strident critics of the central Confederate government and a foe of its attempts to encroach on matters Brown considered the state's purview. *Courtesy of the Library of Congress.*

Lumpkin. But while Cobb himself stayed aloof and vented no apparent ill will, his supporters turned the atmosphere corrosive, and a rift developed between Cobb and Alexander Stephens that rippled through the later secession debate and the establishment of the Confederate government.[17]

Brown was regarded as a curiosity by both his friends and his enemies (and there would be plenty of those). A hardshell Baptist, he was never known to have used profanity and was regarded as totally lacking a sense of humor. He was also never known to have used tobacco and was a rare bird in being a strict teetotaler in the often hard-drinking circles of Georgia politics. He took his personal business affairs as seriously as his religion and pursued earthly rewards just as zealously and particularly as the spiritual. Some of his earnings as a young lawyer he had invested in land and mining property in North Georgia, and by 1860, he had a net worth of $45,000, which included sixteen slaves. One friend described him as "a man of iron will." Another acquaintance, during Brown's campaign for governor, told Alexander Stephens he could not vote for Brown. Brown, he said, lacked "open candor and untarnished character in fairness in the transactions of his life (including politics)" and was "a complete demagogue." This latter quality, however, is no drawback for a politician prone to be a populist, and that Brown was. Never completely trusted by the planter class, Brown the political animal was nevertheless as fierce an advocate for the states' rights as he was a champion of the common man. He was elected governor by a significant margin in 1857 and again in

1859. And while some of his supporters might have resorted to the time-honored practice of plying voters with whiskey, there is no evidence that Joseph Brown ever so much as bought a man a drink.[18]

When Brown had emerged as the Democratic nominee for governor, Robert Toombs is said to have asked, "Who the devil is Joe Brown?" Before long, however, Toombs, a Democrat himself since the collapse of the Whig Party, not only knew who he was but numbered him among his political allies. The two would become, along with Thomas Cobb, the loudest voices for secession. The relationship would last, hotter and colder according to the temperaments of the two men, for the duration of the war. During the Reconstruction years, the relationship between the two would sour to the point of their almost fighting a duel in 1872, but by the time Toombs returned to Georgia in early 1863, after serving as the Confederacy's secretary of state and then on the battlefield as a general, the two shared a common view of the Davis government and similarly damned many aspects of the Confederate national government's war effort in general. In this role, Toombs by himself would become one of the key rallying figures for northeast Georgians throughout the war. This early teaming of the two seemed, though, an alliance of convenience and political expediency, for other than in their politics, the two men—the puritanical and teetotaling Brown and the profane and hard-drinking Toombs—could not have been more different.

Robert Augustus Toombs was born on July 2, 1810, in Wilkes County, about four miles outside Washington, the fifth child of Robert Toombs and his third wife. The elder Toombs, a veteran of the American Revolution, came to Georgia from Virginia shortly after independence. He died when the future Georgia firebrand was only five but left his family well provided for. Records show that all the Toombs children received as fine an education as was available in the region at the time.[19]

In 1824, when he was fourteen, young Robert, already well versed in the classics, entered Franklin College in Athens (later the University of Georgia). Soon, the Robert Toombs who for the rest of his life would make men shake with anger, fear or mirth began to emerge. Early in his second year, Toombs developed a feud with two brothers, Granby and Junius Hillyer. By some accounts, the dispute was over a card game, and by others it was over obscene name-calling by Toombs; whichever it was, the brothers "thrashed" Toombs. A short time later, Toombs attacked the Hillyer brothers, the first with a pistol and the second with a knife and a hatchet. In both cases, other students intervened and prevented bloodshed. The next morning, Toombs tried to ambush them again, this time armed with a club and a pistol, but once again he failed to do his enemies real harm.[50]

The Franklin College faculty was shocked by the violent behavior. While the Hillyer brothers got off with a public admonishment, Toombs was expelled. Later, after he wrote a contrite letter to the college president and submitted a petition in his support signed by the members of both the Demosthenian and Phi Kappa literary societies, he was readmitted. "Toombs should have learned his lesson, but he did not," his biographer, William Thompson, wrote of the incidents years later. "In a sense, he never did. Contempt for authority remained a lifelong characteristic." Toombs's college records reveal that he often received warnings or fines for swearing—another lifelong habit—as well as "boisterous conversation" (probably an understatement) in his room; other evidence points to episodes of drinking and gambling. In Athens then, as now, boys would be boys. One account tells of a drunken Toombs and cohorts confronted by a proctor while returning to their rooms. His companions fled, but Toombs stood his ground. "The guilty flee where no man pursueth," he is quoted as saying, "but the righteous are as bold as a lion." The story has the ring of truth because it sounds like the Toombs who would be seen over and over again in years to come.[51]

This was one of the first accounts of Toombs the worse for drinking, a weakness that would frequently surface during his public career, often with costly consequences, most notably his being passed over for the presidency of the Confederacy. By January 1828, however, the Franklin faculty had seen enough. Toombs was expelled, without reprieve. Almost immediately, Toombs enrolled in Union College in Schenectady, New York, where he completed his degree without apparent incident. Then he studied law at the University of Virginia, where minor infractions whispered of his past. After a year in Charlottesville, he returned to Georgia, ranked last in his law school class of fourteen. Nevertheless, he was admitted to the bar and entered practice in Elberton in March 1830, his license signed by the celebrated jurist and politician Judge William H. Crawford.[52]

About eight months later, the twenty-year-old Toombs married seventeen-year-old Julia Dubose, the daughter of a Lincoln County planter. She was quiet and pious—the opposite of her loud and profane husband—but it was a true love match that endured for over five decades through peaks and troughs of fortune that included the deaths of their three children. Indeed, his wife and his friend Alexander Stephens were the only people who ever seemed able to sway the headstrong and difficult Toombs.[53]

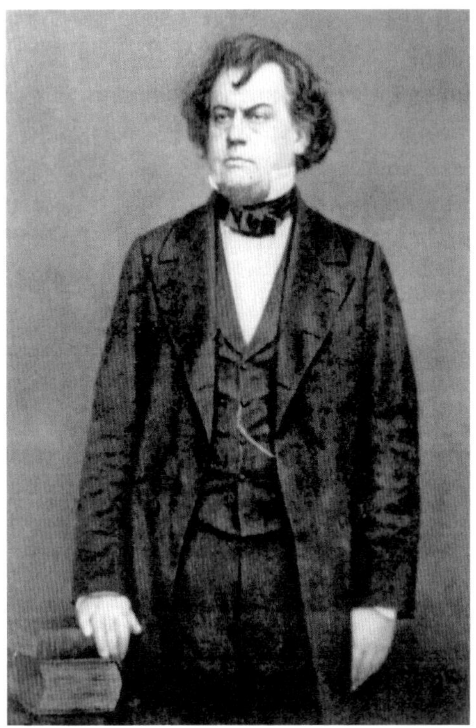

Robert A. Toombs of Washington, Georgia, from a photo taken between 1860 and 1870. As bombastic as he was brilliant, Toombs's was one of the powerful voices for secession. Though he never gave up the Southern cause, later in the war he became one of the Confederate government's most strident critics. *Courtesy of the Library of Congress.*

Bored by the paperwork of the legal profession, Toombs was not an immediate success as a lawyer, but with practice, he shaped his natural bent for oratory into an overpowering courtroom demeanor. He could hone in on the relevant issues and hold his audiences spellbound. Alexander Stephens, possessing a fine legal mind himself, described his friend as a "close and hard student of the law," adding that he had "never seen his superior before judge or jury." Toombs's income rose with his reputation and the demand for his services, and he began to acquire land. By the 1850s, he owned several thousand acres in Georgia, Mississippi, Arkansas and Texas, including the site of present-day Fort Worth, Texas. By the time of the war, he would also own nearly two hundred slaves who worked his Georgia plantation lands.[51]

As it did with Joseph Brown, Alexander Stephens and indeed nearly all of their profession and class, politics beckoned Toombs, and in 1836, he was elected to the Georgia House of Representatives as a Whig. He was a natural politician in the opinion of press observers of the day, described during one daylong political rally in Elberton in 1840 as "fastening the attention of the crowd for between one and two hours by the brilliancy of his wit, humor, anecdote and argument." He was honing his talents for higher office.

In 1844, Toombs was elected to the U.S. House of Representatives, joining his friend Stephens. Again, Toombs and controversy seemed natural companions. In his maiden speech to the House, he attacked the Polk administration's plans to assert control over the Oregon Territory, long a sore spot between the United States and Great Britain. Polk, he thundered, "was the vilest poltroon that ever disgraced our Government" and was determined to bring on a war. To Toombs, Democrats who favored war with Britain were themselves "common sewers to pass those denunciations through this House to the country." In his campaign, he had supported the Whig platform opposing the annexation of Texas for the same reason and, ironically, had been accused of being "soft on slavery" in a time when the battle between free and slave states was already shaping up. Later he, along with Stephens, joined with Abraham Lincoln, then a young congressman from Illinois (for only one term, as it turned out), in opposing the war with Mexico, bitterly contesting what he viewed as the Polk administration's imperialism.[55]

Despite his gift for acrimony, Toombs thrived in Congress—mainly, his biographer Thompson holds, because he was "an excellent raconteur" who intrigued by "spinning his web of charm, bombast and earthiness." Stephens thought his friend a better speaker than Henry Clay, Daniel Webster or John C. Calhoun, "surpassed for raw power only by Niagara Falls." One of Toombs's chief enemies in the debate over the Compromise of 1850 and the issue of the westward expansion of slavery was Jefferson Davis, then a congressman from Mississippi. Yet Toombs managed to make a good impression on the Mississippi congressman's wife, Varina Howell Davis. "One could scarcely imagine a wittier and more agreeable companion," she recorded. He was a "university man, and had kept up his classics. He had the personal habits of a gentleman, and talked such grammar determinately, not ignorantly, as the negroes of this day eschew—unless he became excited, and then his diction is good, his wit keen and his audacity made him equal to anything in the heat of debate...His eyes were magnificent, dark and flashing, and they had a certain lawless way of ranging about that was indicative of his character." As for Toombs and her husband, however, they were "never congenial... but we all went on amicable enough." Such a description leaves a lot unsaid and might give evidence of remarkable restraint on the part of Jefferson Davis. In the aftermath of the fight over the Compromise, Davis lost his bid to become governor of Mississippi and accepted an appointment as secretary of war in the administration of President Franklin Pierce. Toombs continued to jab at Davis, calling him "a disunionist sitting in the councils of the nation," a course Toombs claimed would be taken only by "swaggering braggarts and poltroons."[56]

The Compromise of 1850 was a benchmark for Toombs. In joining with Stephens and Howell Cobb to craft the Georgia Platform that seemed to dampen any enthusiasm for southern secession, he hoped their efforts would put an end to the sectional questions over the spread of slavery to the western territories. In the midst of this fight, however, Toombs foreshadowed his coming shift in viewpoint that he would manifest in 1860. If, he said, the South were driven from the western territories, then he favored disunion. Deprive the South of its rights and "it is your government, not mine. Then I am its enemy…I would swear eternal hostility to your foul domination…I will strike for independence." That was typical of Toombs's bombast at full pitch, but by late 1860, these words would prove prophetic. Like many other southerners, viewing the election of Lincoln against the backdrop of the rise of radical abolitionist sentiment throughout the 1850s, Toombs became a ready advocate for secession. When the Georgia legislature convened in the state capital in Milledgeville on November 7, 1860, some hours before official confirmation of Lincoln's election arrived in the city, Joseph Brown issued his special message to the legislature. He warned of the dire consequences he saw coming to the South and set in motion the machinery that would ultimately end in Georgia's secession. Toombs's booming voice soon joined Brown's.[57]

THE FIRST VOICE OPENLY calling for secession, though, belonged to Thomas Cobb, and it was generally understood, if not publicly acknowledged, that he also spoke for his brother Howell and their political base in Athens and much of the surrounding area of northeast Georgia. For his part, Howell Cobb, somewhat embattled in his position as President James Buchanan's secretary of the treasury, remained in Washington, D.C., and above the fray in Georgia until mid-December. Little brother Tom could carry the fight, and this he did ably.

Thomas Reade Rootes Cobb, thirty-seven years old in 1860, was nearly eight years younger than his more famous brother Howell, but by 1861, he was firmly established as one of Georgia's finest legal minds. A college graduate at age eighteen, he was admitted to the bar the next year, and after practicing law for several years and marrying a daughter of a prominent state supreme court justice, he served as a reporter for the Georgia Supreme Court from 1849 until 1857. In 1858, he published *An Inquiry into the Law of Negro Slavery in the United States of America*, a passionate legal defense of slavery, and the same year sat on the Georgia code commission that drafted the Georgia Code of 1861, the first comprehensive compilation of codified common law to be enacted anywhere in the United States. By the time Franklin College officially became the University of Georgia, Thomas Cobb was helping found its school of law.[58]

Thomas Cobb might have been lauded for his intellect, but he was also regarded by some as arrogant, haughty, conniving, duplicitous and thoroughly unlikable. Before the dust settled in the Georgia secession debates, and especially during the Montgomery convention later to establish the Confederate government, the number of Thomas Cobb's enemies would include both Alexander Stephens and Robert Toombs, even though Cobb and Toombs were allies in beating the drum for disunion. Part of that stemmed from the intriguing of the Cobbs at the Montgomery convention, where Howell would sit as president of the provisional congress, to secure for Howell Cobb the presidency of the Confederacy, a position Toombs also coveted. Thomas served as his brother's stalking horse in the plotting, as he often did, at least as far back as similar intriguing at the national Democratic convention in 1856. When the debate over secession began to heat up in Georgia, Thomas Cobb was back in his old familiar role. For all his bombast in the debate, however, Thomas Cobb entered the fight with a heavy heart. Writing to Howell before Lincoln's election, he had said he felt certain that the Illinoisan's victory would mean the end of the South or of the Union. "I confess I feel sad," he wrote. "The forebodings of my mind are of a most depressing character."[59]

On November 7, 1860, the day that news reached the Georgia state capital of Milledgeville confirming Lincoln's election, Joseph Brown issued his special message to the legislature. He warned of the impending doom that would come from the apparent Radical Republican government, mainly by the appointment of federal officials in the South. These unworthies were either southerners bribed by office or "abolitionist emissaries" who would "eat out our substance, insult us with their arrogance, corrupt our slaves and engender discontent among them." They would do all they could, Brown said, to create conditions that must ultimately result in a war between blacks and whites.[60]

Brown did not call for immediate secession, and that did not satisfy two secession-leaning legislators, who introduced bills that would take Georgia out of the Union by legislative act alone, without a popular convention. On November 12, Thomas Cobb delivered an impassioned speech in Milledgeville that, too, hinted at direct action. The legislature, Cobb said, should "wait not till the grog shops and crossroads shall send up a discordant voice from a divided people," a recklessly indiscreet statement clearly indifferent to any idea of courting popular sentiment. Taking a cue, the legislature's Standing Committee on the State of the Republic proposed a public debate of twenty-four speakers not currently holding seats in the legislature. Toombs and Stephens were among those chosen.[61]

The debate had divided the two stalwart friends in ways that took time to heal. Toombs spoke first, on the night of November 13, and in the words of one historian, he "could not match T.R.R. Cobb's eloquence, but exceeded Cobb's indiscretions." Toombs did not shilly-shally but boldly staked out his own position and role. There was now no choice but to secede, and he was willing to lead the way. "Give me the sword! But if you do not place it in my hands, before God! I shall take it!"[62]

Other celebrated men of long standing in Georgia politics, such as Benjamin H. Hill, gave passionate speeches against secession, but it was Alexander Stephens on the night following Toombs's exhortation to disunion who set the standard. In his thin, often reedy voice, the diminutive Stephens challenged Brown's contention that federal appointments could erode the South's institutions and both Thomas Cobb's and Toombs's assertions that the legislature should act without consulting the people. The Constitution had been made by the people, Stephens avowed, and only they could unmake it. Toombs interrupted Stephens at several points, including here, with his opinion that a popular convention would be dangerous. A convention would, Toombs said, "submit to abolition rule." But when Stephens had finished, Toombs called for three cheers for his friend. "You have just heard," he said, "from one of the brightest intellects and purest hearts in Georgia."[63]

In the end, those wanting a convention got their way, and the campaigning began in earnest. Joseph Brown made a pitch to the roughly two-thirds of Georgians who owned no slaves, most of whom lived in the North Georgia mountain country where Brown considered his political stronghold to be. It was in their best interests, his basic message ran, to preserve the existing order rather than to risk eventual emancipation. The poor whites of Georgia "now get higher wages for their labor, than the poor of any other county on the globe. Most of them are landowners and they are respected," Brown said, in what became a standard speech. The white slaveholders supported high wages for the poor whites because the poor whites supported slavery. If freed, the former slaves would not only become the poor whites' legal and social equals, Brown preached, but also competitors in labor, with a resulting decline in wages. Brown's case was just what was needed, one secession supporter wrote Howell Cobb. Brown's "appeal to the poor men of the mountains [was] well calculated to arouse them," Cobb's correspondent related, "and to fortify their minds against those appeals of demagouges [*sic*] which arouse the basest passions of the human heart, and array the poor against the wealthy—the non-slaverholder [*sic*] against the slaverholder [*sic*]."[61]

One wonders whether Brown was either unaware of or chose to ignore an apparent sentiment of the poor whites against slavery purely on economic grounds that had been rumbling, if quietly, through the undertones of political discussion for over a decade. In 1857, an essentially self-educated son of a North Carolina farmer, Hinton Rowan Helper published *The Impending Crisis in the South*, which distilled this undercurrent into a cogent argument and gave it voice. Helper argued that slave labor, as opposed to a free labor market, was a serious impediment to the widespread development of industry in the South and was a stultifying damper on the economic and social development of the whites not among the planter class. Evidence points to Helper having tapped a rich vein of some rising unvoiced sentiment. In 1849, for example,

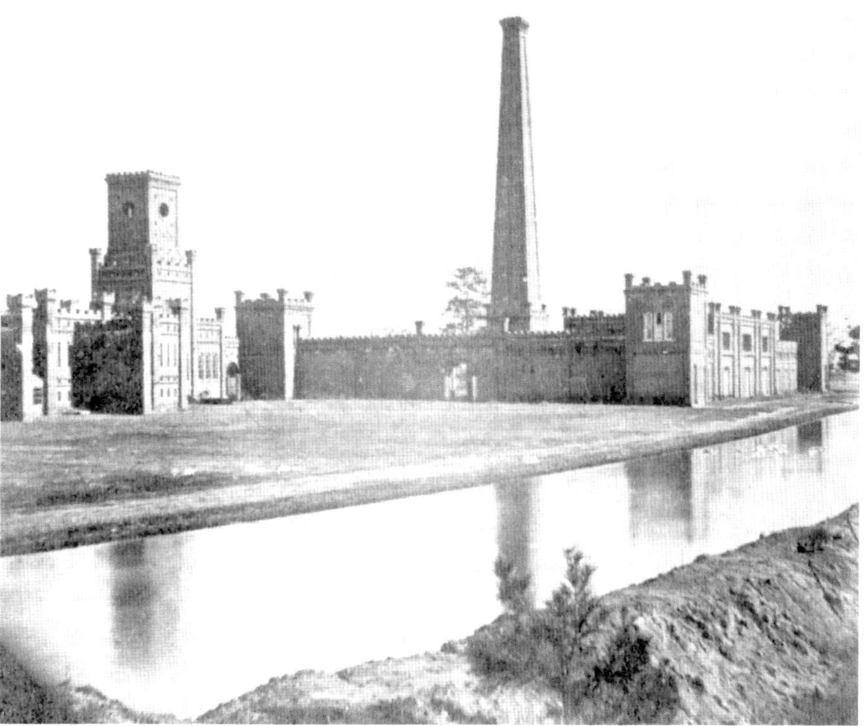

The Confederate powder works in Augusta. At its top production, it produced almost four tons of gunpowder a day, making it the second largest powder factory in the world at the time. Such a target could have lured Sherman's army, which could have brought the war to Georgia's northeast corner in full fury. But the Union army bypassed Augusta, and the mill operated until April 18, 1865. *Courtesy of the Library of Congress.*

a Georgia carpenter vented in print his frustration that having to compete with slave carpenters, whether at work on plantations or hired out by their owners to others, made it hard for him to earn an adequate living. In 1859, in Hancock County, just northeast of the state capital at Milledgeville, a poor white day laborer voiced the same complaint, saying that if it came to war over slavery, he would "black himself" and fight to be rid of it.[65]

Brown's rhetoric was effective, certainly, but not enough to those on the ground to be absolutely confident the hill folk could be won over. Howell Cobb also considered the mountain counties his bailiwick, and it was with no small alarm that Thomas Cobb wired his brother in Washington, D.C., to come home and take their message to the hills himself. The elder Cobb resigned his cabinet post in early December.

The state convention convened on January 16, with a lot of debate still left on both sides. In the end, a resolution for immediate secession passed by a narrower margin than some expected, 166 in favor to 130 against, but an ordinance of secession passed with 208 votes in favor to 89 votes against. The convention also passed a resolution requiring all delegates to sign the ordinance as a show of unity regardless of how they had voted. Six opponents refused.[66]

The lion's share of the votes against had come from North Georgia, from some counties that would see their own localized civil wars between secessionists and Unionists for the duration of the war (and sometimes beyond). In the northeastern section, all of Hall County's delegates voted against secession, as had Pickens, Rabun, Lumpkin and Franklin Counties. Banks County's two delegates had split their votes. Jackson, Habersham, Hart, Elbert, Wilkes, Madison and Lincoln Counties all went solidly for secession. One of Wilkes County's votes was cast by Robert Toombs. (Alexander Stephens, for Taliaferro County, would cast his against the ordinance.) For Oglethorpe County, two delegates went for secession and one opposed. Some delegates were accused of having campaigned under a false flag when, in the end, they sided with the majority. Singleton Sisk, a Baptist minister of E.H. Sutton's native Habersham County, drew heavy criticism in letters to the local editor because he reportedly had campaigned to be a delegate as a Union man but in the voting had gone for secession. All of Clarke County's delegates voted yes, as well, including Asbury Hull, who had been selected as a possible delegate by both camps around Athens.[67]

Others, once they saw the strength of the prevailing wind, resisted as best they could before surrendering to the inevitable. In Lumpkin County, William Martin was a stout opponent of secession and was duly elected one of the county's delegates, defeating his closest secessionist rival by a 50 percent margin. When the convention passed the ordinance of secession, Martin voting no, he offered a resolution to put the question to a direct statewide vote. The resolution was defeated, and Martin returned to Lumpkin County, his duty done. Ironically, with the firing on Fort Sumter and war a reality, Martin became an ardent Confederate, raising money and recruiting soldiers for the cause. Like many who had opposed secession, in the end his loyalty went to his home soil.[68]

Chapter 3

"...Be as Cheerful as Possible..."

The May 13, 1863 edition of the *Southern Watchman* newspaper in Athens published an account of Union cavalry raiding the Western & Atlantic Railroad north of Atlanta, suggesting for the first time in print that Athens and northeast Georgia might be open to the same kind of raid. Except for Fort Pulaski, near Savannah, for Georgians during the first two years, the war had been somewhere else. But the Union armies poised in Tennessee seemed determined to bring it closer.[69]

Athens as a likely target wasn't at all a fanciful notion. The city's factories continued to produce, with the addition of, among others, the Cook and Brother Armory, operated by two English-born brothers, Ferdinand and Francis Cook, who had previously operated a gun manufactory near New Orleans. Escaping the area before that city's fall to Union forces, the brothers had bought and expanded a building on the banks of the Oconee River and went into production in December 1862 with a contract to make thirty thousand Enfield-type rifles for the Confederacy. The plant would produce only about four thousand rifles before the end of the war, with a peak monthly production of about six hundred. It also produced bayonets, horseshoes intended for the cavalry and agricultural machinery such as sorghum mills.[70]

This latter was intended to aid in offsetting a shortage of sugar, one of many shortages of foodstuffs that Athens, like other areas, faced not long into the war. The supplies of salt, beef, pork and grains were never stable, varying from simple shortage; to unwillingness of some who had them to

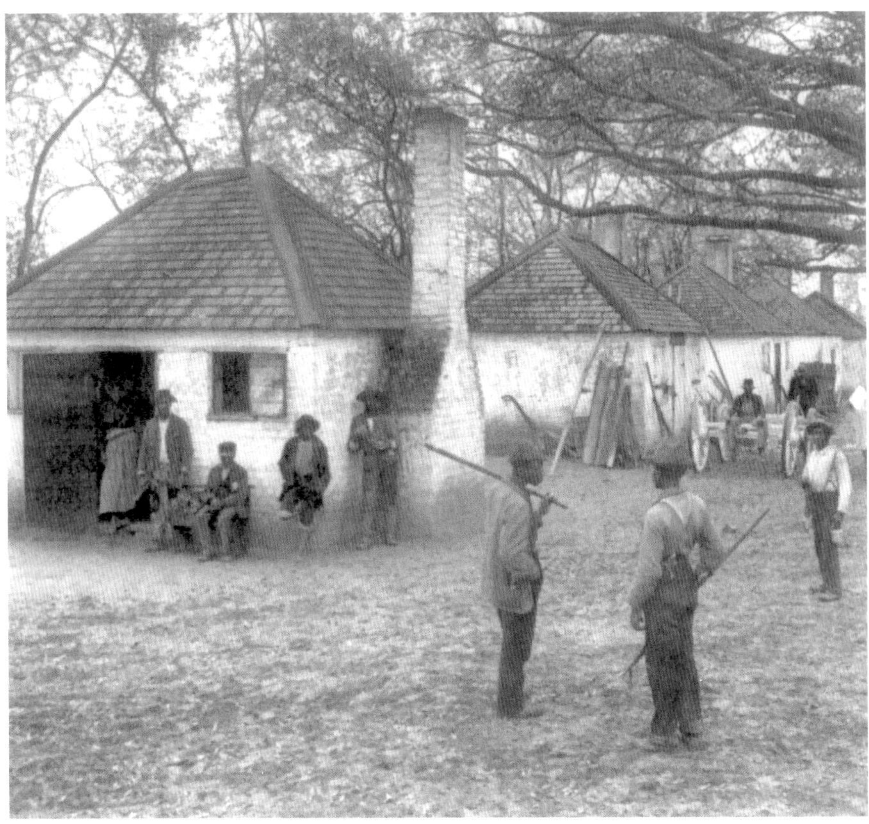

Slave cabins at a plantation near Georgia's coast, from a postwar photo. In middle and northern Georgia, the cabins would more likely be of logs or rough boards. *Courtesy of the Library of Congress.*

sell, except for hard money, gold or silver specie instead of Confederate paper; to competition from Confederate government commissary agents, who could exercise priority in acquiring what was available. And, too, there was blatant speculation by merchants and planters. In a letter to a cohort in April 1862, one merchant was clear on the matter: Southerners, he said, had been "abusing the Yankees for extortion and speculation, but [we are] quite as bad ourselves."[71]

There were no real reported shortages in Athens in 1861, but by 1862, the shortages on the open market of readily available food in Athens were chronic. Curiously, the agricultural South had imported a significant amount of food, such as bacon, from the North before the war, and the lack became keenly felt. Salt became a critical item, needed to preserve any locally produced meat, and was early cut off from Northern trade or import by the Union blockade. The State of Georgia purchased salt from western Virginia to ease the shortage, but by late 1863, it was selling for $125 a sack. Before the war, the same sack had cost $2. Before the war was over, it would be commonplace for the dirt from under smokehouses to be dug out and years of accumulated stray salt recovered out of it. Bacon went from twelve cents per pound in 1861 to fifty cents in 1862. By February 1865, it would cost $4. The $9 barrel of wheat flour became the $400 barrel in the span. Gardens became increasingly important. Those with connections to plantations in other areas, such as the Cobbs, had food brought in. Substitutions flourished. Rice, for instance, could substitute for wheat in making flour. Barley or peanuts could substitute for coffee. By the summer of 1863, the *Southern Banner* would report that okra seeds, dried and ground, made a fine coffee. Real coffee, one of the high-profit-margin items blockade runners could supply, went to $30 per pound early in 1862 and would double by the war's end.[72]

There was, however, a sometimes baffling situation in what was available and what was not. By January 1863, one merchant could not find five hundred pounds of bacon or other pork available for sale anywhere in Athens. The Lumpkin House hotel, however, continued to offer shrimp on its menu well into 1863, along with ice cream.[73]

The state government encouraged the production of food over cotton, even at one point mandating the planting of no more than three acres of cotton per field hand. But not all complied, even after threats of high taxes on excesses, especially some larger planters. Joseph Brown's government instituted a system of indigent relief, with families of soldiers a main target, along with the taxes to support it that vexed some of Brown's political supporters. By 1864, over half the state's spending went to buy food for indigents, but some anecdotal evidence suggests the system became rife with corruption. In some areas, food was more available than others. Some planters raised unusual crops specifically intended for the war effort. In Elbert County, for instance, William M. McIntosh's mother-in-law, Jane Heard Allen, tried her hand at growing ten acres of opium poppies. Combined with alcohol, the raw opium gum would make the laudanum that eased the pain of wounded Confederates.[74]

The threatened approach of Union forces compounded these problems of the homefront. Editor John Christy of the *Southern Watchman* had also proposed a solution along with his warnings—a home guard unit as a more readily responsive supplement to Georgia state troops. On May 25 in Athens occurred the first of a series of public meetings to organize a home guard defense for the Athens area and northeast Georgia. By September, six home guard companies were drilling in Athens, including one composed of the employees of the Cook and Brother Armory, and other units formed in the surrounding area. Most of those serving were either too young or too old for regular service.[75]

A unit of six-month cavalry, the Third Georgia (state militia), formed composed of men from Clarke, Madison, Franklin and Elbert Counties. The cavalry included Judge Thomas W. Thomas of Elberton, who had originally commanded the Fifteenth Georgia, and Amos Akerman, the New Hampshire–born Elberton attorney who had opposed secession but now served as the solicitor general of the Athens circuit. In command was Robert Toombs, commissioned a colonel in the state forces.[76]

Toombs had resigned his commission in the Confederate army months before, arriving in Georgia for good in early 1863. His star had both risen and plummeted, as did nearly every facet of the tempestuous Toombs's life. Incorrigibly insubordinate, Toombs was as despised by his superiors as he was loved, generally, by his men, on whom he appeared, to their thinking at least, to dote. "There has never been but one General Robert Toombs," recalled W.H. Andrews, who served under him as a private. "He would have taken the side of the poorest private against President Davis if he thought he was trying to impose on him. He always defended the weak and helpless. He acknowledged no superiors, and but few equals."[77]

Toombs despised West Point–trained professional soldiers and wasn't shy with his opinion. His own skill on the battlefield was not strategy and tactics but in exhorting his troops. That had served him well at Sharpsburg, Maryland, on September 17, 1862, when two regiments of his brigade had held the rocky heights overlooking what became known as the Burnside Bridge over Antietam Creek. Under the direct command of former Georgia supreme court justice Colonel Henry L. Benning of the Seventeenth Georgia, and with Toombs doing what he did best, about 450 Georgians withstood long assaults from about 12,000 Union troops. Casualties were heavy, but they had bought time for reinforcements to arrive on the Confederate right flank. No less than General Robert E. Lee was reported to have praised Toombs's effort that, arguably, saved the Army of Northern Virginia at Sharpsburg. But in any case, before long, Toombs and the Confederate army had had enough of each other. He would, however, eventually become a brigadier general in the Georgia state forces.[78]

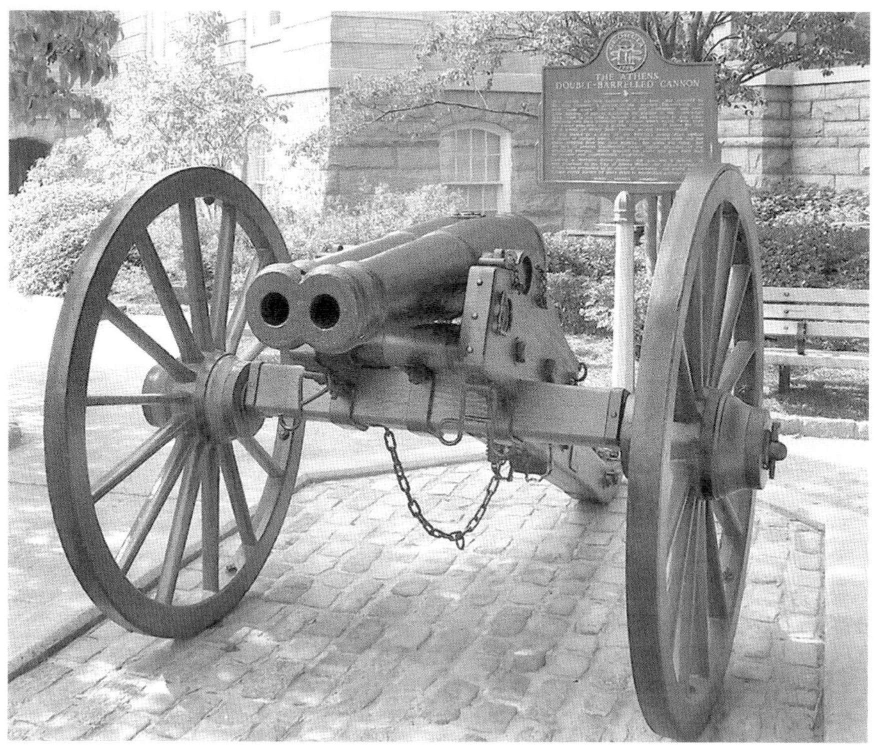

The famous double-barreled cannon of Athens. The dual six-pounder was designed and cast by some innovative citizens who hoped its theoretical ability to throw two balls connected by a chain would aid the Confederacy in sweeping its enemies from the battlefields. Its worthiness proved only theoretical, however, when its field test failed, with the only casualty a cow. It now sits in front of the Athens-Clarke County Courthouse, pointing north. *Author's photograph.*

Toombs's cavalry and the other local units saw no action because the threats of 1863 never materialized. Not all of the companies raised endured. They re-formed in various ways with each call up. The employees of the Cook brothers, however, remained as a unit the longest, as the Twenty-third Georgia Battalion. In January 1864, the state raised what became the Eleventh Georgia Cavalry, actually mounted infantry, as a defense force for northeast Georgia with its headquarters in Athens.[79]

In early July 1864, Howell Cobb, like Toombs not a survivor in the Army of Northern Virginia and now the major general commanding the Georgia troops, made Athens a military post. State troops were soon policing on the streets of Athens, including enforcement of regulations that required passports for visiting civilians. By now threats by Union forces were not speculation but fact. The Union armies of General William T. Sherman had steadily advanced through northwest Georgia in that spring, Atlanta their goal. Athens would be little more than a day's ride for fast-moving cavalry, two days' march for infantry and a likely first target if Sherman turned toward the northeast. By mid-July, impressed slaves were put to work digging fortifications for the city, especially facing west along the Oconee River.[80]

In late July, Sherman sent two brigades of cavalry to destroy the railroad connections leading into Atlanta. One 2,600-strong brigade was defeated by Confederate cavalry west of Atlanta on July 30, but the second, under General George Stoneman, continued southward in a general sweep toward Macon. As a general directive, the Union forces were to free Union officers at Camp Oglethorpe, near Macon, and possibly Union prisoners known to be held at Camp Sumter, near Andersonville. Stoneman tore up rails and burned stations at Covington and Monticello, but a flooded Ocmulgee River that had washed away bridges blocked his way to Macon.[81]

On July 31, Stoneman was attacked at Sunshine Church in Jasper County, and roughly one-third of his force, including Stoneman himself, surrendered near Clinton. Stoneman's men were sent to either Andersonville or Camp Oglethorpe, but Stoneman would be paroled on September 1. That left on the loose two brigades, composed largely of Kentuckians and Michiganers, under Colonel Silas Adams and Colonel Horace Capron, and these burned and pillaged around Madison and Eatonton, twenty miles from the state capital at Milledgeville, and then turned in the general direction of Athens, pursued by Confederate cavalry.

That city had, in fact, been in a state of increased alarm even before the Union rain began. The first warning came at 3:00 a.m. on Saturday, July 23, when some raised the cry that several thousand Union cavalry were twelve miles south of town, at High Shoals. Church bells clanged, and cannon of the local home guard artillery roared their alarms. A mad scramble ensued. Home guard units assembled, though some were reported to have run away with a stream of refugees fleeing east and north. The alarm, though, proved false.[82]

The following Sunday morning at about 11:00 a.m., an unidentified man ran into several churches and announced that Union forces were at a plantation a few miles out of town. Once again, the blast of cannon in front of the city hall sounded the alarm. Churchgoers left "unceremoniously," according to Christy's *Southern Watchman*, and the rival *Southern Banner* agreed: "There was very little apparent excitement, and the congregations retired from their respective churches with their usual order and decorum." John A. Cobb, son of Howell, though, recorded it differently: "All the churches broke up in great confusion & and there was great excitement for some time." In the end, this alarm, too, proved false.[83]

The alarm raised on August 2 was not false. The Union cavalry had taken Watkinsville, the Clarke County seat about eight miles away, that morning without firing a shot. A scouting party stripped some pickets of the Thirtieth Georgia Cavalry Battalion of their uniforms and used them in a ruse to capture an entire seventeen-man guard. "The Yankees came very near getting into town before we believed it," recorded resident Louisa Booth Ashford, writing her son. "Such a scampering out of the way our men had, some on horseback and some on foot in different directions till there was no one left on the street to welcome the Yankees but your pa and Mr. John Harris; they did not attempt to go at all, but talked to them very cleverly, as the Yankees did to us."[84]

Ashford gave the troopers biscuits and later a full meal she cooked, as well as all the buttermilk she had. She opined later that her unforced generosity was the reason she was not forced to cook for them as some of her neighbors were. Troopers did loot her tailor shop but not her house, as they did in several instances. The cavalrymen took almost all the meat and corn they found, as well as other items, including "all the watches they could find." They looted the post office and shops in town, "took all the things they wanted themselves, gave away other things to the negroes, then broke, tore up and destroyed everything else." However, the raiders ignored one general store and the cotton bales stored in the Baptist and Methodist churches and turned toward Athens.

The cavalry had two choices, a road leading to a ford of the middle fork of the Oconee River over two miles above Athens or another that crossed the river below the city. Adams and Capron decided to rush straight for the city, destroy the armory and whatever other material they could find and continue their evasion with their pursuers left with a river to cross.[85]

Athens was in full alarm by 10:00 a.m. Howell Cobb Jr. rushed to find his mother, with other women making bandages at the Soldiers Aid Society, with the news. A scout had reported Union cavalry, maybe eight hundred or more strong, at Watkinsville, headed for Athens. This time there were no bells sounded or cannon fired as the armory workers and three companies of home guard troops formed and prepared to march toward the river crossing. The Yankees, they said, would take Athens only "over the dead bodies of the last one of us." It was quite a contrast to the times before, Mrs. Cobb noted: "Great activity ensued among masculine and feminine, but little consternation or fright—everybody solemn and resolute."[86]

The home guard units, from three to four hundred strong, reached the trenches near the confluence of Barber's and McNutt's Creeks about three and a half miles from town, near the Pioneer Paper Mill, in the early afternoon. One company crossed the creek in a skirmish line. The planking was removed from the bridge. On a fortified line above and behind the trenches, Captain Edward Lumpkin deployed the Wilson Lumpkin Artillery,

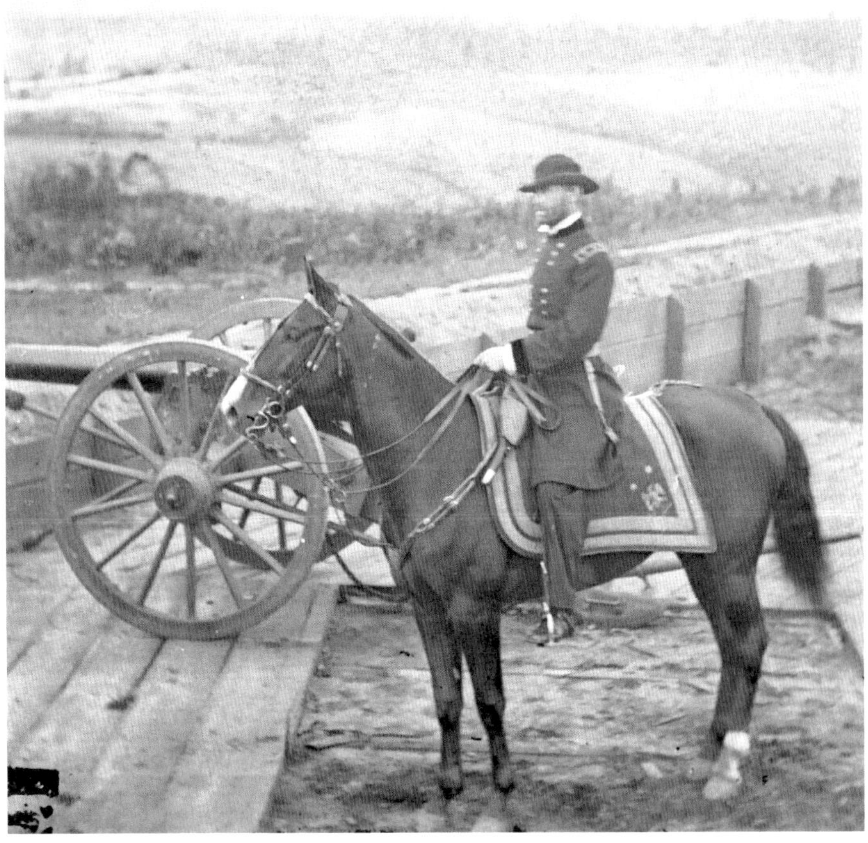

General William Tecumseh Sherman, photographed during the campaigning around Atlanta. The devil incarnate to most Georgians, Sherman's campaign left large swaths of Georgia, such as the northeast corner, untouched but created a refugee problem. *Courtesy of the Library of Congress.*

a battery of twelve-pounders. In the late afternoon, about eighty bluecoat troopers of Adams's command rode into sight, taking station on a hill overlooking the creek.

The cavalry, obviously an advance guard for the eight hundred or more reported in Watkinsville, did not seem inclined to attack. Lumpkin waited and then gave the order for his guns to fire. Four shells arced across the creek and dropped near the troopers. Silas Adams had no answer to artillery and detoured his force westward, sending a courier with the news to Capron.

The Battle of Barber's Creek, as it came to be called, was over. Lumpkin and the home guard companies remained in position for two days in case the Union cavalry made another attempt to attack Athens. None came. Capron took his force along Hog Mountain Road from Watkinsville and met an ambush from Confederate cavalry near Jug Tavern. Capron and a few of his men escaped, but a large share of his force was captured. Adams and his force eluded the Confederate cavalry and returned to Marietta.[87]

Only 209 of Capron's men made it into Athens, but not as invaders. The prisoners taken at Jug Tavern were taken to Athens as a way station to Andersonville. They were penned on the college campus, just off Broad Street, and became a temporary curiosity. "With the excuse of going to a prayer meeting crowds of women gathered in the campus to see the Yankees and talked with them," recorded Mrs. Howell Cobb. "What sort of people are we?"[88]

Northeast Georgia would see no more blue-coated invaders until the war's very last days, but to many, it seemed that the most immediate enemies were former neighbors and the Confederate government itself.

The northernmost mountain counties of Georgia were, for the most part, never really at peace throughout the war, even before the first man of Sherman's armies crossed into the state. Very early, some who rejected secession and the Confederate government formed guerrilla bands and fought any impingement of the Confederacy. Often this degenerated to simple retribution toward secessionist neighbors and, in some cases, to politics providing an excuse for looting, pillaging and murder. One Lumpkin County minister, Josiah Woody, declared that "a line of robbers extends from Rabun County west of the Cohutta Mountains...They are robbing soldiers' families. They broke open many houses and stole rifle guns and money and clothes and provisions to a great extent and soldiers' wives... and even ministers of the gospel have been threatened and badly abused."[89]

Men who wore the gray, or had, could be just as predatory, civilians found. A Lumpkin County militia officer complained mightily when a band of Confederates traveled through the county in 1863 "stealing everything they could get their hands on." Deserters from the Confederate army also found ready hiding places in the northern hills and in some cases joined in the roving gangs. In January 1863, citizens of the Dahlonega area worried about an armed group, estimated to number fifty, "who have deserted from the army...openly proclaiming to resist the laws...and threaten to burn our town." They did burn the home of the outspoken Reverend Woody. Ironically, a week after that, Woody's own brother was arrested for being part of a plot to break a deserter out of the local jail.[90]

Joseph Brown answered appeals from Woody and others in January 1863 by ordering Georgia Line Troops into the hills to combat the armed bands. Confederate troops from Atlanta were ordered by the Confederate secretary of war to join in. Five hundred Georgia and Confederate troops were in Lumpkin County by the end of January. Guerrilla warfare, however, was the fate of the mountains for the duration of the war.[91]

The locals, however, did not always leave matters to the authorities. In November 1863, Lewis Pickford of White County's Mossy Creek community was shot and killed while out with others hunting down a band of roving brigands. A few days later, one member of the band, a Hall County man named Jake Wofford, was captured. Stood on a raised board under a tree limb with a rope around his neck, Wofford refused to name any of his compatriots. Someone among the captors "jerked the plank from under his feet and left him suspended by the neck. In a few minutes he was launched into eternity." Wofford's brother, a loyal Confederate, was reported to have described his brother's hanging as proper justice.[92]

The core of northeast Georgia was spared the worst of such cases. But as the war wore on and Sherman's armies advanced, captured Atlanta and moved across the state, there was no escaping the fact of growing Confederate desertion. The soldiers tired of war sometimes banded together to resist their arrest or sometimes just returned home. This added to the already present resentment and resistance to Confederate government policies of impressment and conscription.

Impressments simply allowed government agents to take whatever was needed for the war effort, even slaves for needed labor, paying set prices in increasingly worthless Confederate paper currency. In October 1863, for instance, impressment agents came to Athens and used troops stationed locally to seal off all roads leading out of town. They then set about seizing all horses of quality, paying from $250 to $600. Editor Christy criticized the seizure as heavy-handed, adding that most would probably have cooperated without force. Two of the horses seized were blooded carriage horses belonging to Mrs. Howell Cobb, but her son John interceded to get them released.[93]

As the war moved toward its concluding months, people's resources grew scarcer and Confederate money grew less valuable than clean writing paper, the possibility of active resistance grew greater. In February 1865, Colonel George W. Brent, assistant adjutant general of the Confederate forces in Augusta, dispatched Major Norman W. Smith, inspector of field transportation, to impress twenty wagons and 80 mules each from Elbert, Oglethorpe, Clarke and Greene Counties. Prosperous Wilkes County would have to contribute thirty wagons and 120 mules and Taliaferro just ten wagons and 40 mules. They were needed to run a freight line from Abbeville, South Carolina, to Washington, Georgia, where the army was establishing a supply depot. "As this mode of proceeding is at all times harsh and calculated to irritate [*sic*] and annoy," Brent wrote in his order, "you will select for this duty your best officers and instruct them to proceed with all possible delicacly [*sic*] and abstain from all conduct which may needlessly vex and alienate the affection of the citizens." The mules and wagons would be returned to the owners when the army no longer needed them, but payment for impressed articles was by now a problem. "As you are without funds and cannot proceed strictly according to the impressment law and the orders regulating the exercise of powers under it, you will proceed, in the [way] indicated by the law, to ascertain the value of the property impressed, and will then give a certificate to the owner, setting forth the time and place, when and where taken, the character and description of the property and the amount of compensation fixed," Brent ordered. "As far as practicable in the discharge of this duty you will conform to the orders regulation impressments." Brent's order also placed a regiment of cavalry at Smith's disposal to help enforce the impressments if necessary.[94]

The Confederate conscription law, though, from the beginning caused problems in Georgia, and the northeast corner was no exception. The Confederate Congress passed three conscription laws over the course of the war, each compounding the reasons men chose to resist. The first, in April 1862, made all men between the ages of eighteen and thirty-five liable for three years of service. The amendment, in September 1862, extended the age limit to forty-five, effective in July 1863. A further amendment in February 1864 stretched the ages from seventeen to fifty-five. Men in occupations considered essential—such as telegraph operators, railroad workers, civil officials, millwrights, blacksmiths, millworkers, state and Confederate civilian employees and plantation overseers, among others—had exemptions. Later, an exemption was added for any man who owned more than twenty slaves. Initially, a conscripted man could buy a substitute, but this practice was halted in December 1863 as public sentiment and resistance grew over the conscription law's almost shameless unfairness. "Owners of twenty hands ought to be made [to] fight for their property or be deprived of it," one soldier wrote home. Another conscripted Georgia soldier wrote a neighbor, "They've got me in this war at last. I didn't want to have anything to do with it anyhow. I didn't vote for Secession—but them are the ones who have to go & fight now—and those who were so fast for war stay out."[95] Another wrote that even those who had voluntarily joined found their enlistments extended by the law and "are today slaves—nay, worse than slaves—bruts [*sic*]—chained under the yoke of military discipline and must abide their time."[96] Very early, conscription officers met resistance and a growing antiwar feeling by those whose war blood had cooled or who had wanted no part of the fight in the first place.

William H. Andrews, who served with the First Georgia Regiment, recorded that "conscript officers [are] stationed everywhere I go, watching for some poor devil who is trying to keep out of the army. If he cannot be caught any other way, [the conscript officer] will run him down with Negro dogs and take him to the front in chains."[97] If, that is, the conscript officer could stop his prisoner's friends from freeing him for force.

Joseph Brown sympathized with those Georgians with rising gorges over conscription, but he had additional reasons for stridently opposing the law, both philosophical and practical. It was a gross violation of constitutional and state's rights, in Brown's view, and also left the state vulnerable. "No act of the Government of the United States prior to the secession of Georgia," Brown wrote, "struck a blow at constitutional liberty so fell as has been stricken by the conscription acts." Thousands of Georgians had flocked to the Confederate army, Brown said, and would continue to, but the Confederate national government had no authority to conscript. If the Confederate government conscripted "all between thirty-five and forty-five as conscripts, you disband and destroy all military organization in this State and leave her people utterly powerless to protect their own families even against their own slaves."[98]

In November 1862, the Georgia Supreme Court ruled in *Jeffers v. Fair* that conscription by the Confederate national government was constitutional.

March 18, 1865.] FRANK LESLIE'S ILLUSTRATED NEWSPAPER. 405

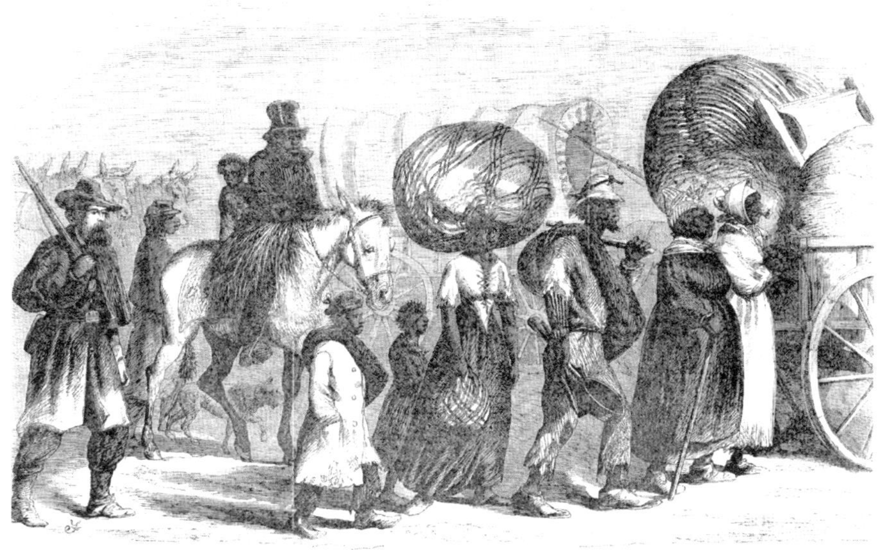

CONTRABANDS ACCOMPANYING THE LINE OF SHERMAN'S MARCH THROUGH GEORGIA.—FROM A SKETCH BY OUR SPECIAL ARTIST.

As Sherman's army marched across Georgia, legions of freed slaves, labeled "contrabands," often traveled in the Union army's wake, generally to Sherman's annoyance. Journalists traveling with the army plied their drawing pens to record the scenes. *Courtesy of the Library of Congress.*

The Confederate Constitution provided for the raising of an army. Voluntary enlistments were the ideal, but nothing in the constitution prohibited conscription if it was decided necessary.[99] That did not decide the matter, however, because many state court judges, not uncommon at the time, did not feel unconditionally bound to accept supreme court decisions as the final word. One of those was Judge Thomas W. Thomas of Elberton, the Fifteenth Georgia's first commander and later a volunteer in Toombs's state cavalry, who was the first state court judge to declare conscription unconstitutional. He rejected the decision of the court and continued to fight the law in his court until his death in the spring of 1864.[100]

Early on the heels of the first law in April 1862, Thomas had ordered the arrest of an enrolling officer, Joseph Glenn, in Oglethorpe County, who had arrested a conscript, Richard Fleeman, in Elbert County and removed him by force from the county after Thomas had issued a writ of habeas corpus. The case arose when Fleeman, noticing the exemption in the law for civil officials, contrived to have himself elected as a justice of the peace. Glenn pressed the issue, considering the expedient as evasion. Thomas reasoned based on a 1830s state case involving a writ and a free black: "Is an alleged conscript to be denied the benefit of this writ, and it is to be given to free negroes and to bushmen with tails? Is a conscript a slave?"

Thomas was concerned enough about possible open conflict with Confederate authorities that he contacted Joseph Brown. Brown, already at war with the Davis government, did not enter the fray but did put local state troops on alert in case Confederate authorities tried to free Glenn by force. In the end, though, Glenn's superior released Fleeman.[101] The writ of habeas corpus was the chief weapon of judges such as Thomas in combating conscription officers. In Thomas's reasoning, the military had authority over soldiers but the local courts had the authority to decide who became a soldier. The writ opened the inquiry into the alleged shirker's status. Thomas, in fact, would free every conscript who appeared before his court.[102]

By one estimate, by October 1862, over half the soldiers from northeastern Georgia had deserted and were hiding in the hills, including at least one-third of Lumpkin County's Blue Ridge Rifles, who had marched out of Dahlonega in June 1861, each with a gift of a new Bible in his hand. By the final months of the war in the spring of 1865, the problem of deserters and conscription evaders posed such a crisis that neither the Confederate government nor Joseph Brown could ignore it. According to accounts, some deserters or stragglers posed as impressment agents, backed by purported military force, to seize whatever they wanted under supposed authority of the Confederate government.[103]

In December 1864, Brown requested that Brigadier General William T. Wofford, a Habersham County native recuperating at home in Georgia from wounds received with the Army of Northern Virginia, be made commander of the military district of North Georgia with a special warrant to raise troops to combat lawlessness. A Mexican War veteran, Wofford had opposed secession but had remained loyal to his state, compiling an admirable combat record in the Army of Northern Virginia's campaigns. He had, in fact, taken over the command of Thomas Cobb's brigade, including the Twenty-fourth Georgia, in which E.H. Sutton served, after Cobb's death at Fredericksburg in December 1862. He would take his new command in January 1865.[104] On December 23, 1864, a directive issued over Brown's signature boldly reinforced previous efforts to keep the peace. Brown directed the state's reserve troops to carry out patrols and give all necessary protection to civilians with special attention to the homes of soldiers' families, protecting them "from depredations of thieves and marauders." They were also to arrest all men under fifty years of age liable for service, as well as to arrest "stragglers and deserters" and send them, if Confederate, to the provost or, if state troops, to the nearest camp.[105]

Other troops were meeting resistance from generally law-abiding citizens who took umbrage at what they saw as political oppression. In the first week of January 1865, some residents of Jackson County met to request a state convention calling for a negotiated peace to end the war. Both Hart County and Lumpkin County had already done the same. Others would do so.[106] The Jackson County meeting was broken up by Confederate cavalry under Brigadier General Jesse Glenn. Glenn reportedly told the group the meeting should not take place "unless he was satisfied the people intended to pass 'the right sort of resolutions.'" Editor Christy of the *Southern Watchman* called Glenn's action "an outrage upon the constitutional rights" of the people of Jackson County. "There was scarcely a man at that meeting who had not lost a son, a brother or some dear relative in this cruel war," Christy opined. "There was not a man there who had not been taxed to the last cent and the last peck of corn he was able to spare to support, in idleness, the very soldiers who were brought there to over awe them!" The best evidence that the Jackson Countians were still loyal, Christy said, was that they had not shot the soldiers for interfering with them. Christy published letters from Jackson citizens asserting their right to hold the meeting and demanding to know whether Glenn acted on his own or under orders, all the while complimenting the general on his own gentlemanly conduct. That point remained unclear.[107]

On March 7, in Clarkesville, Habersham County residents held a meeting with no overtures for peace. The actions of the Union forces left no room for negotiation, the Habersham Countians resolved, and "we hereby renew our vows to the cause of independence and liberty until the same are secured."[108]

Other citizens riled at some of the supposed guardians sent among them. In February 1865, Colonel T.T. Dorough was authorized to raise a company of fifty men to patrol Jackson, Banks, Habersham, Franklin, Hart, Elbert, Madison and Oglethorpe Counties. Dorough was to arrest all deserters and stragglers he met. In early March 1865, the Madison County grand jury protested Dorough and his men coming through their county "with no apparent prospect of doing good, and with every appearance of distressing the county and damaging the cause of the country." There were few, if any, deserters among them, the Madison Countians protested, and they could at

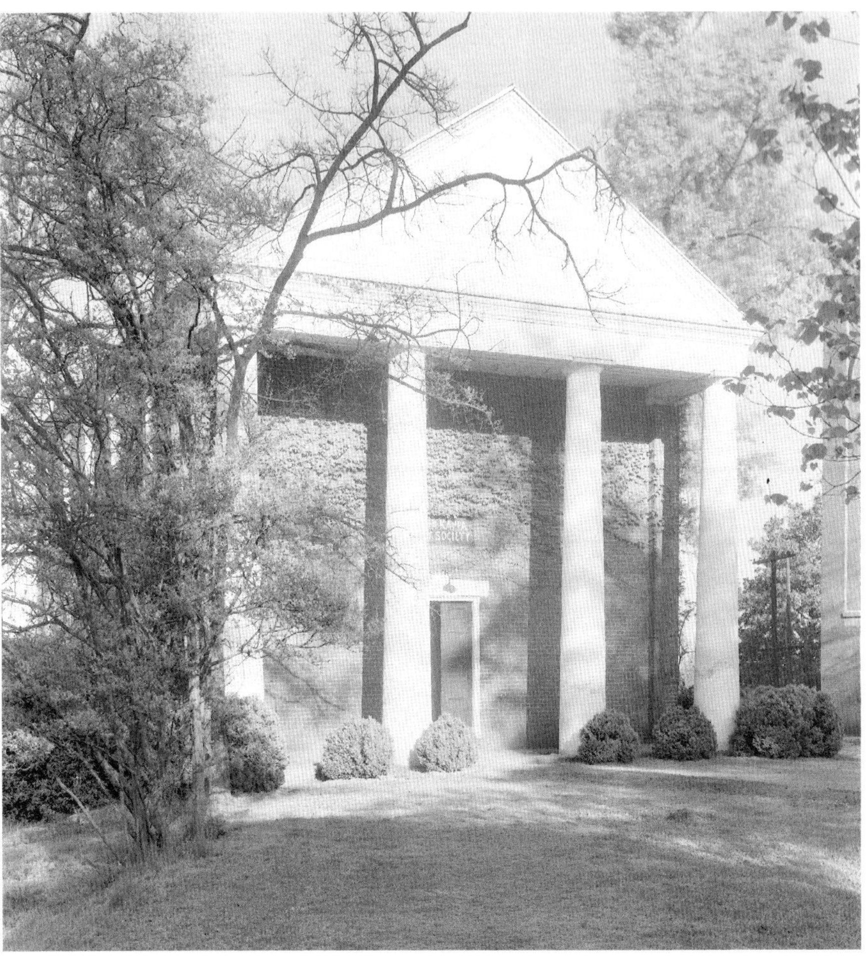

Phi Kappa Hall, on the University of Georgia campus in Athens, home of the Phi Kappa literary society. The Union forces occupying Athens reportedly used the lower story as a stable. *Courtesy of the Library of Congress.*

any rate police themselves. A few weeks later, a group of Elbert Countians published a defense of Dorough. The cavalry had arrested "quite a number of deserters and outliers, who up until that time had evaded the enrolling officers and the vigilance of the police." The Elbert Countians could recall no incident in which the men had interfered with any civilian property or anyone with the proper papers or had not respected civil law. How one tended to view the roving provosts depended on a mix of circumstances, sometimes particular, just as with how civilians viewed returning Confederate soldiers who perhaps had not been formally discharged. There is no record, for instance, that anyone objected when a group of soldiers returning to Hart County in early March from the Army of Tennessee broke into a gristmill's warehouse near Hartwell and distributed government cornmeal and flour to hungry civilians.[109]

Other communities had clearer reasons for resenting the provost's patrols, reasons that, in one case, led the citizens on the grand jury of Franklin County on April 6 to question what the war had been about. Some weeks earlier, a Georgia state cavalry patrol passing through Carnesville had shot and killed a resisting soldier later found to the Franklin Countians' satisfaction not to have been a deserter. The civil authorities demanded the sergeant commanding the patrol hand over the troopers who had killed the man. The sergeant refused and, according to the grand jurymen, declared that military law trumped civilian law, mounted his men and rode out. The jurymen appealed to the state troops' commanding general, Howell Cobb, asking that the killers be surrendered. "If squads of cavalry passing through our county are to be allowed to commit the most brutal acts of murder and other crimes, without being liable or subject to the civil laws of the country...we think we have fought the war to but little purpose."[110]

WARREN AKINS DIDN'T WANT to leave his family on their own in the summer of 1864, but while his heart lay with them in Elberton, his duty lay in Richmond. The fifty-two-year-old Akins had been elected in the fall of 1863 to represent Georgia's Tenth District in the second Confederate Congress, and the fall session was at hand. He had relatives in Elbert County, where he had been born, and it seemed a safe place to lodge his family.

Akins had left Elbert County as a youth. He had decided early that he wanted to be a lawyer after, it is said, having been awed at the age of ten by a court proceeding he observed. But at age eighteen, he was a clerk at a store in Monroe, in Walton County, when he heard of the gold strike in Georgia's mountains not far away to the northwest. He headed for the gold fields, where by all accounts he did well. He was also studying law books, though, and was admitted to the bar in Cherokee County in 1836. Almost immediately, he moved to the village of Cassville, in what later became Bartow County. He married and was widowed, and in 1848, he married again, to Mary Frances Verdery. By 1860, his net worth was nearly $70,000, which included several slaves.[111]

Like many lawyers, he was drawn to politics. A staunch Whig, he had been an elector for that party in 1840 and in 1850 was a delegate to the state convention that had heartily endorsed the Georgia Platform of Toombs,

Stephens and Cobb. In 1859, he had run against Joseph Brown in Brown's throw to win a second term as governor. Like many Whigs, he had opposed secession but had dutifully followed the decision of the state. He represented his county in state legislature from 1861 until 1863, serving also as Speaker of the House. Then in the fall of 1863, he sought election to the Second Confederate Congress.[112]

Only one of Georgia's ten representatives to the lower chamber of the Confederate Congress in the first Congress was reelected to the second. The others were either defeated or declined to seek a second term. In later years, that turnover was interpreted as a general dissatisfaction with the way the war was going and with the Davis government in general. Modern, more probing inquiries, though, take a different view—that it was not a repudiation of the Davis government, which had acted in many ways to raise the public pique, including the suspensions the Congress had authorized of habeas corpus. This had been especially vexing to both Joseph Brown and Alexander Stephens, who even as vice president became quickly disaffected with Davis. (With Brown, Stephens would lead the fight in Georgia for the legislature to pass a bill, introduced by Linton Stephens, condemning and declaring void Richmond's suspension of the time-honored principle.) Nor was it necessarily an endorsement of Brown's governance of the state, which by late 1863 was seeing Brown put out the first feelers of sentiments for a negotiated peace with the North. (By March 1864, he and the Stephens brothers would be earnestly considering ideas for trying to end the war at the negotiating table.) Instead, the replacement of nine incumbents is seen as an outcome decided by those offended, irritated and outright mad at the sacrifices called on through conscription, impressment and direct taxes such as the "tax in kind" (by which the Confederacy claimed 10 percent of agricultural produce) that were being shirked by some. The speculation by some planters and the "twenty negro" rule that allowed the wealthier planters to avoid conscription gave pause to some who—like grand jurymen of Franklin County would do vehemently in March 1865—reconsidered what they had gone to war for.[113]

Akins, certainly, was no wild-eyed supporter of Brown, nor was he an opponent of the Davis government. During his eighteen weeks in the Confederate Congress, from November 28, 1864, until late February 1865, he would prove one of Davis's most reliable allies in Congress.

The certainty of a Union advance into northwest Georgia prompted Akins to move his family to Oxford, near Atlanta, in January 1864, but as Sherman's armies swept irresistibly toward Atlanta through the spring of 1864, it was clear to Akins that his family needed to seek refuge in an area likely not to be a target. Elbert County it would be. He moved them there in August 1864: his wife; his thirteen-year-old daughter, Eliza; and his four sons, Elbert, Thomas Warren, Henry Clay and John Wesley. His wife was pregnant with yet another child. A daughter, Susie Henry, was born in Elberton on October 24, 1864. They found many other refugees from the war-torn parts of Georgia in Elbert County and also found themselves among friends.

"We are among very kind people here," Akins wrote a friend on October 31. "They have aided in feeding us to a great extent since we have been here." He went on to describe that, among other things, friends had given him a cow for milk, eggs, two hams, lard and butter, sacks of white and sweet potatoes and a demijohn of sorghum syrup, in addition to some cloth for clothing. He had rented a place in the Middleton community, east of Elberton, of about seven acres, five of which he wrote he planned for his sons to farm in corn or wheat. The rent was costing him $800 for a year, but, he wrote, the place had some fruit trees and a fine well. It was a good place to leave his family, which he did in a matter of days after writing that letter, because he was in Richmond, in Congress, on November 28, albeit three weeks after the session had started.[111]

That day, he wrote his first letter to his wife. He was appalled at the prices in Richmond, in particular the twenty-five dollars a day it cost him to stay at the American Hotel. An apple had cost him one dollar, and a cup of coffee, a piece of bread and a roasted partridge at a restaurant cost twenty dollars. Milk at ten dollars a quart—"and half water at that"—and butter at twelve dollars a pound he would do without. It would take most of his pay just for his board, he opined, so he advised his wife to ask a neighboring farmer named Overton Tate to rent them twenty acres for growing corn the next year and another ten or fifteen acres suitable for sowing in oats. "Do your best on him—tell him how necessary it is for us, etc., etc."[112]

Mary Frances Akins's letters back to her husband kept him well informed of her progress in keeping his wishes and reflected her own problems in managing her small part of the Confederate Georgian homefront. She had not only her children and the rented farm to oversee but also from six to eight of the Akins family's slaves. (The number of slaves that traveled with the family to Elberton isn't clear from the letters.) In time, she would hire out two of the slaves, Floyd and Charles, for three hundred pounds and two hundred pounds of pork, respectively, for her family's larder plus board for the slaves from their employer. She would keep Bob, who Warren Akins intended would farm the additional land rented from Overton Tate. With Bob, however, she had problems, which she communicated to her husband, in that he was becoming lazy, willful, independent-minded, slow to follow instructions and "as mean as possible" about any task given him. So had Charles been, according to her letters to her husband, a main reason she had been eager to hire him out to someone else. "He is so lazy and disobedient I can do nothing with him," she wrote of him. "I don't believe I ever saw as lazy a negro as he is. If Gilreath [a neighbor] cannot hire him out what must I do with him? I have written you how uneasy I feel about your being in Richmond now."[116]

Mrs. Akins's problem with the slaves was a common one across the wartime South, one that grew stealthily the nearer Union armies drew. The South's wartime footing—with many of the practices of the prewar plantation system turned on their heads, including reductions in some areas of the manpower available for the rural area slave patrols, the "paterrollers" of slave lore—translated often into less direct oversight. This was often more the case in urban areas than in rural. In many cases, the only real result was almost an early taste of freedom with an aftermath that was benign. When Mrs. Howell Cobb left Athens in late 1861 to spend time at her brother's plantation near Macon, she left six house servants behind to essentially fend for themselves. One woman, Aggy, who could write, kept their mistress apprised of their situation. Aggy took in sewing, another woman took in washing and a man named Ben hired out for day labor so they could buy flour, meal and other foods to supplement the three barrels of salted beef they had been left to eat. Mary Cobb was happy with the arrangement. "All they can save from their support is their own," she wrote in late March 1862 to her husband, Howell, then with the Confederate army in Virginia. "All I required of them was to take care of the house and lot—and a cow & calf and make me a garden in the spring."[117]

Many Georgia cities saw blacks flock to their streets as the war wore on and especially as Sherman's armies moved south and inhabitants became refugees, as did the Akins family. Sometimes, there were no owners evident, often the case when a slave had been impressed for some work related to the war effort or had been hired out. In September 1864, a newspaper article in Macon described the city as "filled to overflowing with negroes, many of whom are here without their owners, and but few if any are in possession of passes." They were hiring out and "demean themselves generally as if they were free people." City leaders were called on "to look after the drove of negroes in our midst and find out by what authority they have located here."[118]

One response was to tighten the laws and ordinances on written passes, which were always required even in the years before the war when slaves were away from their owner's property or out and about after certain hours but now further restricted. General passes that could be held and used more than once would no longer suffice. Passes now had to specify the owner and where the slave was allowed to be and between what hours. In some cases, this proved difficult to enforce when some owners ignored the stiffer laws and gave trusted slaves general passes anyway. In other cases, city police forces, even beefed up with volunteers, were either still too small to handle the problem or not necessarily inclined to see it as a crisis. In Athens, for example, city marshal B.B. Moon was thought to not be overly concerned with enforcing the city's early tightened ordinances pertaining to slaves when his January 1862 reelection as marshal was reportedly celebrated by from fifty to one hundred blacks "throwing their caps up into the air and hurrahing at the very top of their lungs." By late 1864, Athenians were venting the same complaints as residents of Macon, Augusta and Savannah that the slaves found on the streets were "impudent," no longer gave way to whites on sidewalks and were "rather obnoxious."[119]

In the 1930s, a New Deal program sent writers out to interview surviving slaves, recording their memories as a historical and cultural resource. The oldest from the northeast and central Georgia area was Adeline Willis, of Wilkes County, who at the time she was interviewed in May 1937 reckoned her age at about one hundred. Like a surprising number of other former slaves from northeast and central Georgia, she recounted her masters and mistresses as kind and caring, demanding of discipline and seldom accepting less than complete obedience but also generous. Willis remembered food as always plentiful and generally few material wants. Other slaves of less

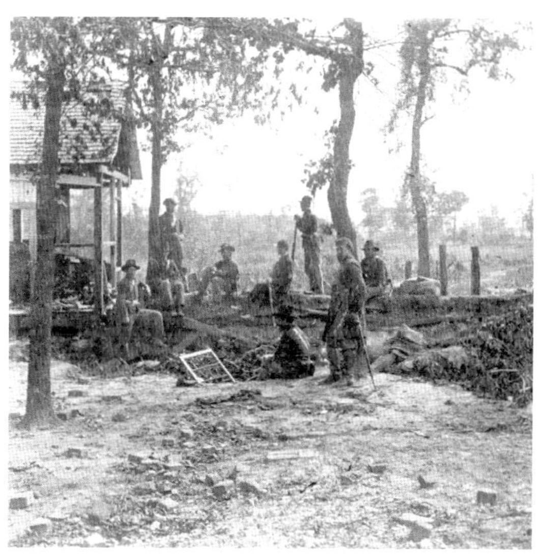

Union soldiers encamped near Atlanta, late 1864. Only in the last days of the war did most northeast Georgians see a Union soldier. *Courtesy of the Georgia State Archives.*

prosperous owners did report scant rations on more than one occasion, if not as a rule. Just as some reported owners who would readily sell slaves to slave dealers, even breaking up families without remorse, other owners were reported never to have sold slaves or separated married slaves or a couple from their children. There was no typical one sort of slave owner any more than, it can be said, there was any one typical kind of slave. But the South's wartime footing turned so much of the plantation system inside out that the relationship between master and slave became a casualty of war. Where there had often been plenty before the war, now there was want. The demands of the war sapped supplies of food and clothing, and the economic woes of the Confederacy, especially its rapidly depreciating currency, made purchases of whatever there was difficult for many planters. For many planters, there was little choice. They could not maintain their chattel property. By the middle of 1864, Augusta residents, for example, complained that blacks were crowding into the city, reported to have been released by their owners. Without any apparent means of support, they were readily suspected of any theft of food or clothing. Even where the owners did not expressly release their slaves, some apparently gave up all caring whether the slaves ran away, so long as they would be rid of any responsibility for their care. Adam Alexander, father of Porter Alexander, was a master known before the war for his care of his slaves. His plantation issued new clothes for winter and summer, the winter clothes of more expensive wool. By 1863, however, osnaburg had replaced wool for winter clothing, and the summer clothing issue had been reduced by half. By late 1864, he had decided not to provide new winter shoes at all. "Then," he wrote to his daughter of his decision, "if any of our people run to the Yankees, we shall save the shoes at least."[120]

It is not evident from Mary Akins's letters that she encountered serious problems with the family servants beyond a lessened willingness to work and an independent streak given freer rein. There was certainly nothing that justified her apparent fears that made her uneasy about her husband's absence. No doubt she had heard of incidents such as from near Athens in July 1862 in which a slave had attacked an overseer's wife. He was dragged from the jail and hanged by a group of citizens. In 1863, a slave near Atlanta had met the same fate for raping an eleven-year-old girl, his body left hanging to rot as a warning to others. A slave charged with rape near Macon in February 1864 was luckier, in a fashion. He escaped hanging but was castrated instead. His fate, wrote the editor of the local newspaper, would also serve as a warning to others. It's very likely accurate to say that the Akins family slaves had heard of these incidents as well.[121]

Warren Akins's letters home gave no real indication that he grasped the changing nature of the master-slave relationship in northeastern Georgia and everywhere else. He never seemed to read between the lines of his wife's letters for any unelaborated fears. His advice was to be firm with Bob. "When you want Bob to do any thing, don't ask him, but order him," he wrote. And if Bob were to continue to leave without her permission, he advised, she was to tell him, "I will certainly punish him if I live to get home."[122] For the most part, his letters were filled with concerns over the cost of being in Congress and how his family would also manage. He wrote on December 18 that he was wearing a shirt and his socks all week to save laundering costs. A dollar apiece for washing socks, he thought, was too much. "I intend to save all I can because it is necessary in order to be able to live through the war…Do your best in everything, for it is very uncertain when I will be able to get home." He always laced his concerns with detailed instructions for managing their rented farm; as diligent as Akins was to the business of the Congress, his long and frequent letters show his every thought not on his duties to Congress was on his family and how they would survive the war and the aftermath. His eldest son, fifteen-year-old Elbert, would not. Elbert died in February 1865, three days after a serious fall from a horse. Akins would never know of his son's death before he returned home. He obtained leave from Congress in late February and started for home. There is no clear reason recorded for his leaving Congress so early, but his letters clearly show that his greatest concerns were at home. Warren Akins reached Elberton on March 5.[123]

One of the people in Elbert County with whom Warren Akins did business by letter and through his wife's direct dealing was William Mattox, brother-in-law of William McIntosh. Akins was troubled that Mattox would not accept Confederate bonds in payment for five hundred pounds of salted pork, for which Mrs. Akins had paid $1.50 per pound. Where the Akinses had lost their home in Cassville and were eking out an existence as refugees, Mattox, it could be said, had a good war.[124]

William Henry Mattox was born on January 5, 1836, in Elbert County, the son of Henry Page Mattox, a planter and onetime state legislator. In 1852, young William was sent to Franklin College, the future University of Georgia. He made the best of it despite having no scholarly ambitions. In later years, he would make a great impression on others with the depth and breadth of his education. Graduating in 1856, he soon began laying the foundation of what would become his own empire. Probably with his father's backing, he acquired land in Elbert County along the Savannah River near the mouth of Beaverdam Creek. In 1858, he bought three hundred acres at Cherokee Ford on the upper Savannah, and the next year, he added more than seven hundred acres to his holdings. Along the way, he also acquired seventy-nine slaves.

Mattox also made the time-honored good move of marrying well. In 1858, he wed Rebecca Allen, a daughter of Singleton Allen. Singleton's father, William, had established a prosperous plantation and mercantile business along Beaverdam Creek in the 1790s, coupled with some business interests in the then-thriving river port of Petersburg, a town at the confluence of the Broad and Savannah Rivers. Singleton himself had married well, his wife, Jane, being the daughter of Stephen Heard, a local hero of the Revolution and a onetime provisional governor of Georgia. Their other daughters married William McIntosh and Young L.G. Harris.[125]

In the summer of 1861, Mattox was elected second lieutenant in the McIntosh Volunteers that William McIntosh formed. He kept this rank when the volunteers became Company I of the Fifteenth Georgia Infantry Regiment. On Christmas Day 1861, he was promoted to captain. Soldiering, however, really didn't seem to agree with him. As early as September, he had become ill.

"Bill Mattox has not held up as well as I have," McIntosh wrote Young Harris on September 26, 1861. "He is even now under the weather, not confined to his bed but complaining. I got him into a house not far from camp, where he is doing well, and I hope will soon be able to return to duty."

McIntosh's words hinted that Mattox was a malingerer. At the time, the Fifteenth Georgia was stationed in Northern Virginia, in the vicinity of the Manassas battlefield, where it remained for a good portion of the winter of 1861–62. The regiment was involved in skirmishing on occasion, but there is no record of Mattox being involved or even present. Well before the real bloodbath in Virginia began in earnest with the Seven Days Battles in June 1862, Mattox resigned his commission. He had been home for some time before McIntosh met his own death on the battlefield in late June.[126]

Accounts of Mattox's activities on the homefront suggest that he intended to become a prosperous man in the midst of poverty. To do so, he exploited the shortage and dearness of hard money in the South at a time when Confederate currency became more worthless every day.

During the war, Mattox borrowed $10,000 in gold specie from Mildred "Miss Millie" Gray, a local lady of some wealth who was related to Mattox by marriage. Miss Millie had inherited considerable property and money from her deceased first husband, Beverly Allen, the brother of Singleton Allen.

Having so much hard money at hand was unusual for even most wealthy Georgians in those years, but by family accounts, the brothers Singleton and Beverly Allen had, like Warren Akins, ventured into the North Georgia gold fields around Dahlonega and Auraria to increase the family fortune.

In the 1930s, an elderly descendant of Mrs. Gray recounted playing on old gold mining machinery the brothers had brought home and stored in a barn. In fact, the specie Mattox borrowed might have been coins minted in Dahlonega, but that is speculation. Whatever the source of the coinage, the loan wasn't repaid in kind. Mattox did repay the obligation before the end of the war, but he did so with depreciating Confederate currency. As late as the 1930s, descendants of the Gray family retained bundles of worthless Confederate money Mattox had paid to Miss Millie.

As a result of these investments, Mattox spent money when most Georgians, like the Akins family, were struggling to survive. Even in September 1865, he and two partners bought a substantial tract of land along Beaverdam Creek that included a gristmill. Mattox would pay $4,859 in gold.[127]

Chapter 4

"We Knew Then, We Had 'Gone Up'"

Eliza Frances Andrews reached her home in Washington, Georgia, on Friday, April 21, 1865. She and her sister Metta had had a harrowing trip from her married sister's home in southwest Georgia across a landscape in panic at advances of Union cavalry from the west. Refugees clogged every town; finding a place on the few remaining trains operating was difficult, and the overland transport was worse. They were finally reduced to a hired cart pulled by a mule too frazzled to be of interest to a government impressment agent.[128]

The two had traveled part of the way more or less under the care of Robert Toombs, who was making his way back to Washington, before Toombs opted for a more direct overland route with the help of military transport furnished by Howell Cobb, then commanding what state forces still existed. On April 16, Cobb's forces, outnumbered over three to one and including Toombs with a small command, had been defeated in trying to prevent Union forces from capturing Columbus in what is often regarded as the last battle of the war. Toombs, at least, was now going home. Eliza and her sister crossed paths with Joseph Brown, who met them "with no pretense of cordiality," which Eliza wasn't sure whether to mark down to her father's well-known Unionist feelings or Brown's evident preoccupation with problems at hand. In any case, she wasn't impressed by Georgia's governor, who sported a "rusty short-tailed old alpaca coat that had a decidedly home-made set." In face, Brown wore "an expression of self-assertion rather than obstinacy and I couldn't help thinking how he would have fitted in with

Cromwell's Ironsides." The Andrews sisters had learned both of Lee's surrender of his army and of Lincoln's assassination on the trip and were uncertain what they would find at home.[129]

The train up the spur to Washington, she noted, was crammed with former Confederate soldiers. It would be a sight she would get used to in coming days and weeks. "When we drew up to the depot, amid all the hustle and bustle of a military post, I could hardly believe this was the same quiet little village we had left sleeping in the winter sunshine five months ago," she noted. Government wagons filled the streets, and she saw squads of soldiers everywhere.[130]

One of the soldiers she saw could well have been twenty-three-year-old John S. Jackman, of the Ninth Kentucky. A schoolteacher before the war, Jackman's regiment was part of the Kentucky Brigade, the so-called Orphan Brigade, earning that label because Kentucky never seceded, though some of its citizens—most prominently former U.S. vice president, presidential contender and Confederate general John C. Breckinridge—had. Jackman had arrived in Washington on April 18, joining others of his brigade there with a special duty to guard the brigade's boxes of records. These they stored in a building being used by some of their brigade as a saddle factory. It was easy duty under the

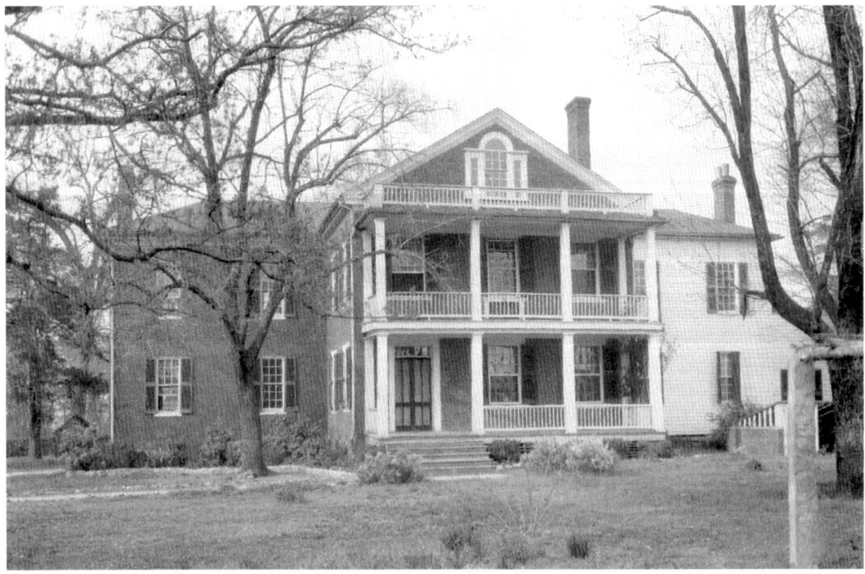

The Gilbert-Alexander-Wright Home at 312 North Alexander Avenue, Washington, Georgia, in a 1934 photograph. *Courtesy of the Library of Congress.*

circumstances, and Jackson found Washington "well built, and in a better country than usual, for Georgia." The people he found aristocratic.[131]

"We had not been in Washington but a few days, when Lee's paroled men commenced coming through," Jackman recalled. "From that time on, the streets were full of soldiers." Then the news came of the surrender of General Joseph Johnston and the remnants of the Army of Tennessee to Sherman in North Carolina. "We knew then we had 'gone up.'"[132]

Others knew it, too, in Jackman's estimation, because what little order and discipline remained was breaking down. On one occasion, he witnessed the troopers of the Eighth Texas Cavalry, on their way west, loot forage from the commissary depot, following up by breaking into the army quartermaster's warehouse, where they "threw out writing paper, thread, buttons, etc., on the streets by the wagon load. The little negroes and villagers soon had wheelbarrows on the ground to take the plunder home." The quartermaster's guards had refused to fire on men they still considered their own, but eventually they were able to restore order, after which Jackson witnessed the entertaining spectacle of the guards "chasing the little negroes about for some time, on the streets, making them 'shell out' the stolen goods."[133]

Eliza Andrews was visiting a friend when the riot broke out, and she started home by way of the backstreets, hoping to avoid it all. But she met stragglers at every turn, their arms loaded with their loot. "The soldiers were very generous, giving away paper, pens, tape, etc., to anybody they happened to meet." One soldier shoved a ream of paper at Andrews, telling her to use it to "write my sweetheart." Reaching home, she found the family's servants toting up their own booty. With the depot pillaged, she reasoned, the continuing flow of homeward-bound Confederates would find little left in government stores for sustenance, which would throw more of the burden on the townspeople.[134]

The next day, another group of renegade Confederate cavalrymen raided the depot and left piles of powder and ball cartridges scattered around, with once again the civilians helping themselves. "I expected to see the Depot blown up, by carelessness," Jackman recalled.[135]

Texas Confederates, especially, lost much of the sympathy and goodwill from the locals through their simply taking whatever horses or mules were available in civilian hands. "There is hardly a planter in Wilkes County who has not lost one or more of his working animals since they began to pass through," Andrews noted. On one occasion, a neighbor's stable was broken into at night, and on another, the Texans took two horses "from the buggies of quiet citizens on the square."[136]

Like other houses in Washington, the Andrews house was overrun with guests, for no one was refused if there was room. So, too, with the meals, even when the food was sometimes only field peas and ham, with a cake sweetened with sorghum for dessert, a fact that shamed young Eliza when she remembered the meals of better times. Still, when her father gave a dinner for General Arnold Elzey and his staff, the table was set with the best china and silver. "But it was all in absurd contrast to what we had to eat."[137]

Ex-Confederates continued to pack the town, ragged, starved and filthy. "The sidewalk around there is alive with vermin, and some people say they have seen lice crawling on the walls of houses. Poor fellows, this is worse than facing Yankee bullets," Eliza noted. At a spring on the edge of town where the soldiers washed, the townspeople noted lice crawling on the grass around and stopped walking there themselves. Still, these soldiers who came begging seldom went away without something. Despite his Unionist views, Eliza wrote, her father never refused a hungry man. Two family servants (always referred to as servants by Eliza, even when they had been slaves) were set to fixing rations while, sometimes, the eager young Eliza talked to the homeward-bound men. "Some of them, as they talked to me about the surrender, would break down and cry like children." On one occasion, such a display of emotion got the men all the family's lard and eggs laid out for that day's meal, "for I could not bear to see them eating heavy old biscuit made of nothing but flour and water. In that way a good part of our supper was disposed of before we sat down to it, but nobody begrudged the loss." Only once did she record a party going away without being fed. A group of cavalrymen rode up as the family and guests were seated at the table and asked for a meal. There being no room at the table, Mrs. Andrews directed that a table be set up on the porch. It angered the cavalrymen that they were not invited inside. They rode away cursing that Judge Andrews was a "damned old aristocrat, and deserved to have his house burned."[138]

On Saturday, April 29, Judge William Wood Crump became a guest at the Andrews home. An "ugly old fellow, with a big nose, but perfectly delightful in conversation," in Eliza's estimation, Crump was also both the president of the Bank of Virginia and the assistant secretary of the treasury for the Confederacy. At that point, he had been on the run for almost a month.[139]

In mid-March, in the Confederate government's waning days, the State of Virginia had authorized a loan of $300,000 in hard currency to the Confederate government, to be backed by two million pounds of cotton. The three banks that handled the state's finances—the Bank of Virginia, the Farmer's Bank of

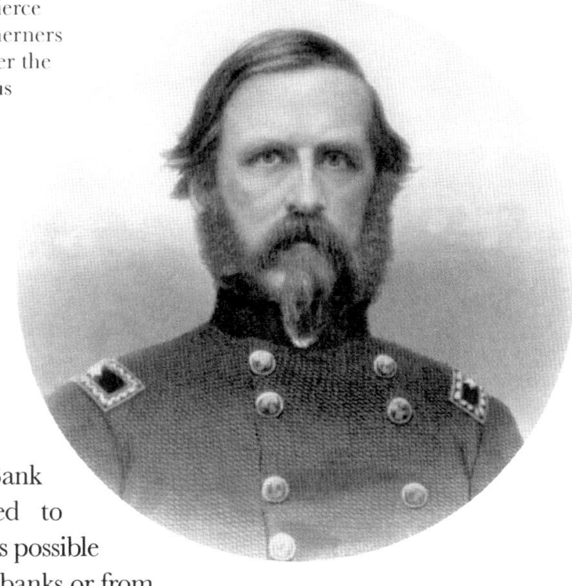

General Edward A. Wild. A fierce abolitionist, Wild hated Southerners with a passion. He would order the torture and arrest of Dionysius Chennault and his family members in an attempt to recover the gold and silver of the Richmond banks. He would later be associated with the Freedmen's Bureau. *Courtesy of the Library of Congress.*

Virginia and Exchange Bank of Richmond—scrambled to assemble as much specie as possible for the loan, from smaller banks or from private holdings. But as it became more evident that Richmond was doomed, the Confederate Congress adjourned and fled the city before authorizing the loan's surety. The banks were left holding $450,000 in gold and silver.[110]

In the early hours of April 2, Union forces besieging the Army of Northern Virginia at Petersburg, twenty miles to the south of Richmond, breached the Confederate lines, and Robert E. Lee ordered his army to evacuate Petersburg, setting the men on a westward path. The army had another week to exist as it trekked toward Appomattox Courthouse. Lee had signaled Jefferson Davis that Richmond, too, must soon fall. Crump and his cadre of bankers also intended to move the money somewhere.

Crump knew that the Confederate government intended to move what remained of the hard money in the Confederate treasury and intended to try moving their money with the official funds. Richmond was a bedlam, a city knowing that enemy occupation within hours was certain. Through this, Crump and staff from the banks moved the money to the Richmond train depot, where the Confederate treasury was being loaded aboard one of the last trains to leave.

The Confederate treasury, about $327,000 in gold and silver specie, reportedly including English gold sovereigns and Mexican silver dollars, all bagged and packed in coin boxes, was under the guard of Lieutenant William H. Parker of the Confederate navy. Parker, born in New York but a Virginian by heritage, was thirty-five years old and had served in the U.S.

Navy before the war. For most of the previous year, though, he had been superintendent of the Confederacy's naval academy, which consisted of a refurbished mail packet, the CSS *Patrick Henry*, as a training ship and some buildings along a Richmond wharf. On the Sunday morning of April 2, Parker received orders to bring his corps of midshipmen, who ranged in age from seventeen to twelve, to the Richmond-Danville train depot that evening at 6:00 p.m. and report to the quartermaster. Only then was he told that he, his few adult staff and his midshipmen were the guards for the Confederate treasury and the funds of the Richmond banks as well.[111]

So began an odyssey for Parker and his band of adolescent guards, with their retinue of Confederate treasury clerks and Richmond bankers. At first, Parker stayed roughly with the fleeing government of Jefferson Davis and the cabinet officers who had joined him, who first settled in Danville, Virginia. But later he moved on to Greensboro, North Carolina, and then on to Charlotte. He hoped at every stop to be relieved of his responsibility but could find no one in authority willing to take on his burden. Trying to telegraph Secretary of the Navy Stephen Mallory from Charlotte, Parker learned that Union general George Stoneman's cavalry had taken Salisbury and was heading generally southward. Stoneman, paroled and exchanged after his debacle in middle Georgia in late 1864, had been ordered to sweep south with his whole new command in an effort to catch Jefferson Davis and his traveling government. Since the assassination of Lincoln and rising suspicion of official Confederate involvement, catching Davis—who was rumored among the Union troopers to be traveling with a Confederate treasury rumored in some Union army dispatches to be as much as $13 million in gold—was a top priority.[112]

All that Parker knew, however, was that his little command and its charge were in danger. After talks with the treasury clerks and bankers, he decided to move south, maybe, he wrote later, as far as Macon, Georgia. He left Charlotte with a stronger guard, now including a group of armed men from the Charlotte Naval Yard, as well as a wealth of rations from the Charlotte naval warehouse. He also left with Varina Davis, who had traveled ahead of her husband and who Parker now urged to leave Charlotte, and the approaching Union cavalry, under his protection. It might have helped his case that Mrs. Davis's younger brother, Joseph, was one of Parker's midshipmen.[113]

When the rail line ran out in Chester, South Carolina, Parker switched his command to wagons for the overland trip to the next railhead at Newberry, from there to go to Abbeville, South Carolina. In Abbeville, Parker's command moved overland to Washington, crossing the Savannah River on a pontoon bridge into the southeast corner of Elbert County before taking the road to Washington. The farther he traveled, Parker later wrote, the worse the news of the Confederates' situation became, and he hastened the pace. "We 'lightened ship' as we went along—throwing away books, stationary [*sic*] and, as we heard worse news, Confederate money." In Washington, he learned of Lee's surrender and resolved to go to Augusta. It wasn't, Parker wrote later, that he didn't feel he could defend the treasury; it was that he did not want the moral responsibility for the money. He did not find his relief in Augusta, however, where treasury officials refused to take charge of it. Parker received a telegram from Secretary of the Navy Mallory ordering him to disband his command. This he refused to do as long as he had responsibility for the Confederacy's hard money. Fearing Augusta was vulnerable, he decided to move back to Washington, and then farther if necessary, and turn the treasury over to Davis himself. He left Augusta but without Crump and the Richmond banks' gold. Crump had decided to remain in Augusta for the time being.[114]

Parker did reverse his track as far as Abbeville, about forty-five miles from Washington, where Davis arrived early on the morning of May 2 with a cavalry escort of several hundred men of General Basil Duke's command and what remained of his cabinet entourage, joined since the flight from Richmond by John C. Breckinridge, now the most recent (and last) Confederate secretary of war. Davis had arrived as Parker was considering another run back to Newberry, having heard that Union cavalry was raiding nearby Anderson. He turned the money over to Davis and disbanded his command.[115]

In Augusta, meanwhile, after Parker left, Crump had second thoughts. He decided to move his hoard back to Washington. This time not taking the Georgia Railroad spur to Washington, he and his bankers moved the gold overland by wagon, arriving in Washington on May 3. Crump housed the gold in the Bank of Georgia building on the square.

JEFFERSON DAVIS ALSO RODE into Washington on the afternoon of May 3, escorted by the remnants of the Second Kentucky Cavalry, Duke's command. His party had lost most of its escort after crossing the pontoon over the Savannah River in the day's earliest hours. A loud majority of the troopers of the escort, knowing the war was over, demanded to go home. But they also wanted to be paid and well knew what Parker had transferred to Davis's keeping in Abbeville. Some threatened to now seize the money, which they thought likely to fall into Union hands anyway.[116]

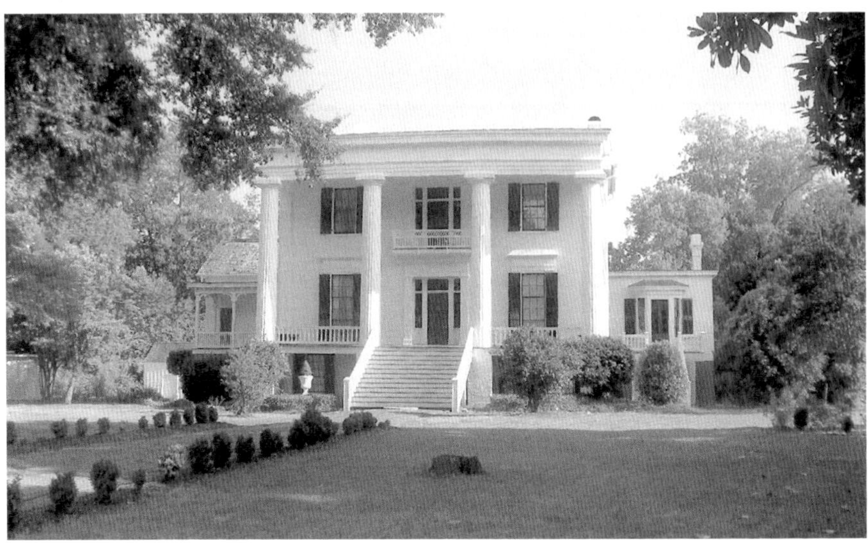

The Washington, Georgia home of Robert Toombs. Toombs would flee a side entrance of this house in May 1865 as Federal troops entered the front door to arrest him. He would ultimately end up in Paris, France, before finally returning to the United States. *Author's photograph.*

Two versions of what happened come down. In the official version, Breckinridge, commanding the escort, had each man who wanted to leave paid. The thousand-odd troopers received, by the official accounts, twenty-six dollars each in silver. But the accounts of the treasury, made by Captain Micajah Clark, with Davis's party, show also that a total of just over $108,000 was disbursed at the riverside, reducing the treasury to about $143,000 (treasury clerks had exchanged some specie for citizens' Confederate paper on earlier stops along the way, decreasing the original amount). In the other, more likely account, the payoff began orderly but became almost a looting there in the circle of wagons drawn up on the Georgia shore just before dawn. One officer who observed the scene later recorded that "they were impatient, and helped themselves as soon as they discovered where they could get it." As a result, the officer said, some got much, some got little or none and some coins got trampled into the dirt, leavings for others to find.[117]

Davis entered Washington ahead of his escort, with little fanfare despite about forty of his staff following. He wore a broad-brimmed, light-colored hat with a band of black crepe, a gray coat without any markings and cavalry boots, recalled John Jackman, who saw him ride into town. "I had never seen him dressed like that before, but I knew him the moment I saw him. He dismounted at the old bank building, on the square, near where we were staying. Nearly all his cabinet was with him." General Elzey and others on the bank building porch, where some boarded, also recognized him and took off their hats in respect. The bank would also serve as Davis's refuge during his brief stay in Washington.[148]

A young officer staying with the Andrews family ran to ask them for food for Davis and his party. "There was not a crust of bread in the house, every available thing having been given to soldiers," Eliza recalled. But a group of soldiers waiting for bread baking in the Andrews kitchen were willing to give it to Davis, and with milk Eliza begged from a neighbor as well as what had been intended for the Andrewses' and their guests' own supper, Davis and his party were fed. An exhausted Davis slept but, after waking, was counseled by many, including General Elzey, that he was traveling too openly. Rumors were rife that Union cavalry combed the countryside for Davis. The counselors advised he travel with a smaller party.[149]

The stream of visitors that flocked to the bank to see him was evidence enough that he attracted attention. One visitor was Garnett Andrews, who, though an opponent of secession, offered Davis every comfort within his means. "Father says his manner is so calm and dignified that he could not help admiring the man," Eliza wrote.[150]

Robert Toombs, however, did not come and did not offer Davis the hospitality of his house, perhaps four hundred yards off the square. He sent Davis formal greetings and an offer of help, including help in getting out of the country if Davis chose, but, as Toombs wrote later, "I could not receive him in my house." The bitterness between the two, from Toombs's perspective, ran too deep. Toombs had called on Varina Davis during her earlier sojourn in Washington, offering her every kind of help he could offer, but meeting her husband face to face again was another matter. In fact, Varina Davis's last recorded glimpse of Washington as she rode out had been of Toombs. He had been standing beside a buggy in the street amid throngs of refugee soldiers "in an ill-cut Websterian coat the worse for wear, his face concealed under a broad-brimmed black hat." But it was unmistakably Toombs, for he was making the morning air "murky with blasphemies and denunciations of Yankees."[151]

Davis rode out of Washington about 10:00 a.m. on May 4. Earlier, he held his last cabinet meeting in the bank building and disbanded his government. He had also authorized the final disbursements of the Confederate treasury, which included $86,000 that a naval officer, James A. Semple, was to attempt to smuggle out of the country as a reserve for further Confederate resistance.

A total of $40,000 in silver was paid out to a commissary officer to buy food for Confederate troops on their way home. Breckinridge and General Braxton Bragg, Davis's chief military advisor in the last days, received funds for their intended flights to the Confederacy's Trans-Mississippi Department, where Davis had some hope of continuing the war.

Davis left town with only one companion, Eliza Andrews noted. His cavalry escort, now reduced to ten volunteers, had gone on ahead. When he emerged from the bank building, he found a crowd waiting, some of the women bearing flowers. He thanked each woman individually. Some noted the shadow of tears in his eyes. There were certainly tears in the eyes of some of the other men, including General Elzey, who, Eliza recalled, pretended that he had dust in his eye. British journalist and illustrator Frank Vizetelly, who had been traveling with the Davis party and had come to admire the Confederate president, made his last sketch of Davis there in the square, saying his goodbyes to the townspeople and his former escorts. "With tears in his eyes," Vizetelly recalled, "he begged the men to seek their own safety and leave him to his fate."[152]

Edward Porter Alexander arrived back in Washington a few hours too late to see Davis leave. The thirty-four-year-old Alexander, a brigadier general at the war's end, had been one of the officers at Robert E. Lee's right hand on the march to Appomattox and, before the laying down of arms, had urged Lee to disband his army to scatter and fight a guerrilla action. Lee, however, had been concerned that Southerners had as much or more to fear from the depredations of a mob now stripped of military discipline turned loose upon the land as they had to fear from Union soldiers. No, he told Alexander, he had no other honorable course except surrender. Alexander, for his part, had resolved even before the surrender to try to make his way to Brazil and offer his military experience to that country's government, embroiled in conflicts of its own.[153]

After leaving Appomattox Courthouse on April 12, he went to Washington, D.C., despite the urgings of some Union officers he had served with before the war and were now renewed acquaintances that, in the wake of Lincoln's assassination before he arrived, it was not a safe city for a known ex-Confederate. He could have saved himself the risk. Alexander found the Brazilian ambassador there unhelpful in his quest. His next jump was to New York City to see the Brazilian consul, who was also unsympathetic to his aims. He did, however, buy his wife as much as he could carry in dress goods that had been scarce in the Confederacy. He took a packet boat to

Hilton Head Island and from there made his way back to Washington. He arrived on the afternoon after Davis had left and met for the first time the daughter his wife had given birth to on April 7.[151]

On May 5, the first Union cavalry, the Thirteenth Tennessee (Union) Cavalry, rode into Washington. The next day, John Jackman's comrades in the rest of the Kentucky Brigade arrived. As they marched in, rifles shouldered, Confederate battle flag flying, they passed a line of the Thirteenth Tennessee Cavalry headed in the opposite direction. "It looked strange not to see them commence shooting at each other," Jackman recalled. He would work all night getting the men's parole paperwork in order and would leave for home himself on May 8.[155]

Eliza Andrews also witnessed the passing of the troops. "There were several companies of negroes among [the Union troops], and their hateful old striped flag was floating in triumph above their heads." Some turned their back on the scene, she recalled, and at least one woman shook her fist at the bluecoats. She said she wished the flag had been trampled into the dust. "My father took me by the shoulder and said if I didn't change my way of talking about the flag of our country he would send me to my room

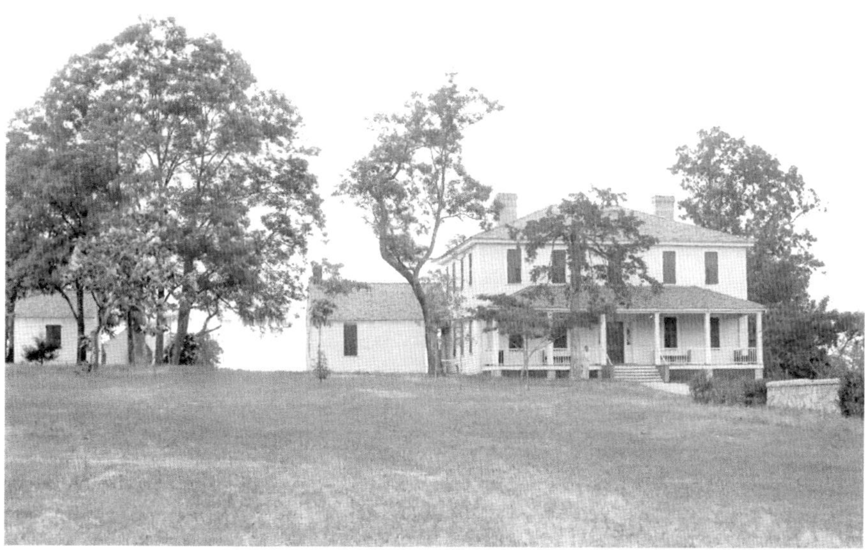

Liberty Hall in Crawfordville, Georgia. Close to Washington, Liberty Hall was the home and refuge of Alexander Stephens. He spent a good deal of his time as Confederate vice president in this house and was arrested there by Union troops in May 1865. *Courtesy of the Library of Congress.*

and keep me there a week. We had never known anything but peace and security and protection under that flag, he said, as long as we remain true to it. I wanted to ask him what sort of peace and protection the people along Sherman's line of march had found under it, but I didn't dare."[156]

Washington was garrisoned by a company of the Fourth Iowa under Captain Lot Abraham. Abraham would generally prove himself a fair occupier, though depredations big and small continued, by both Union occupiers and renegade and desperate ex-Confederates. Washingtonians noted the number of articles they recognized tied to Union saddles. Some just found Abraham's handling of civilian complaints grating. Actions both large and small seemed deliberate salt sprinkled on the wounds of defeat. At one point, ex-Confederates were refused paroles unless they surrendered their horses and arms, which they vowed not to do. They knew of the generous conditions granted the Confederate armies at both Lee's surrender in Virginia and Joseph Johnston's surrender in North Carolina, and they expected the same. Some Union soldiers taunted the townspeople. "I thought you Rebs were all subjugated now and I could go where I pleased," said one soldier asked to leave a house he had simply entered unannounced. One neighbor of the Andrewses requested and received from Abraham a guard to protect his family from predators in either uniform. But Abraham refused to force the guard to stay unless he was allowed to join the family at the table for meals. It was horrible, Eliza Andrews thought, that safety had to be bought at such a price, to have "a horrible plebian of a Yankee, who is fitter company for the negroes in the kitchen sit at the table with them." Eliza, regretting that she had no money except for Confederate, pondered selling cigarettes she had learned from a soldier to roll to the Union troops. "Only," she wrote, "I could not bear the humiliation."[157]

OTHER AREAS AROUND WERE knowing the same treatment. The Thirteenth Tennessee was part of the division of brevet Brigadier General William Palmer, of Stoneman's command that had cut a swath through the Carolinas in pursuit of Jefferson Davis. Palmer's troopers had crossed the Savannah River at Hatton's Ferry, into Franklin County, about the same time that Jefferson Davis's party crossed the river on the pontoon bridge into Elbert County. Palmer believed Davis was headed for Athens, though he also pushed out the Fifteenth Pennsylvania Cavalry southward in case Davis was heading toward Augusta. The Thirteenth Tennessee Palmer sent toward Athens.[158]

As the Union cavalry fanned out across northeast Georgia, panic set in among the Georgians who had heard the tales of looting if they did not know

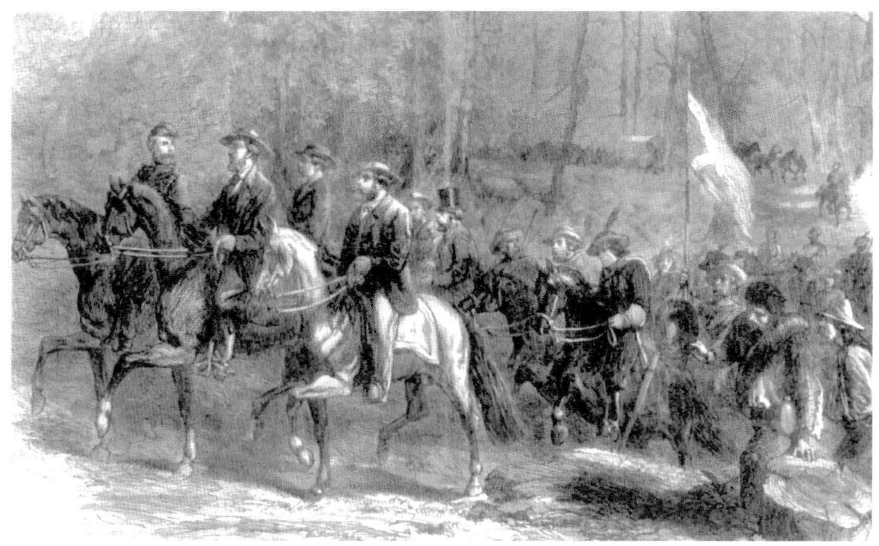

A drawing of Jefferson Davis heading toward Washington, Georgia, after crossing the Savannah River. The illustration appeared in the *Illustrated London News*, provided by British war correspondent Frank Vizetelly, who traveled with Davis's party until the fleeing Confederate president reached Washington. *Courtesy of the Library of Congress.*

it firsthand. In Franklin County, Mrs. William Mitchell, of near Carnesville, took what few remaining pieces of jewelry she had—a cameo, two watches and some gold cufflinks—and tied them up in a knotted green veil. This she tied among the leaves of an apple tree in her yard, where it remained until all danger had passed. In Elbert County, a neighbor drove a buggy up to the home on Beaverdam Creek of Millie Gray, William Mattox's creditor, and asked her to take a quantity of gold coins for safekeeping. No, Gray replied, she had enough of her own to worry about. The neighbor continued on down the road that ran along the creek bank. Gray's home did receive a visit from Union cavalry in the family's lore, and owners of the house pointed out the marks on the door allegedly made by a kick of Union boots that remained for as long as the house stood.[159]

When the Thirteenth Tennessee reached Athens early on May 4, some of the troopers looted with abandon, stripping every watch and other jewelry readily in their sight. Palmer reached Athens with his full command later that day and established his headquarters, arriving in time to quell a raid by some members of the public on a former Confederate commissary. He detailed the Thirteenth Tennessee to Lexington, in Oglethorpe County; to Elberton; and to Washington on a wide sweep in hope of picking up Davis's scent. The regiment was in camp in Lexington when they were called out, searched and twenty-two stolen watches were sent back to Palmer in Athens to return to the rightful, and complaining, owners. The Thirteenth Tennessee pushed on to Washington and was later ordered twenty miles south to Crawfordville, where the officers contacted Alexander Stephens at his home, with his half brother Linton. He expected arrest, according to officers of the regiment, but they had no orders to arrest him. But while they were there, they heard that the Fourth Michigan had caught Jefferson Davis near Irwinville, Georgia, on May 10. Stephens was arrested the next day.[160]

Robert Toombs had been unmolested in Washington through the first days of Union occupation, but that changed at about 1:30 p.m. on May 11, when between thirty and forty cavalrymen rode up to the Toombses' house in Washington. Many of the cavalrymen, by one account, were black.

Toombs, by his own later account, was in his basement study when the cavalry arrived. He headed for the back door as his wife met the blue-coated officers on the front porch. Julia Toombs denied her husband was home and stalled the men long enough for Toombs to reach his horse stabled behind the house and head for the open countryside. "I didn't like the idea of staying in Boston Harbor in Fort Warren, even in the company of Mr. [Alexander] Stephens," Toombs said years later of the escape. "I preferred Paris, so I took my horse and scooted."[161]

The captain in charge of the detail ordered the house searched, to no good, and then the grounds and outbuildings to just as much success. Mrs. Toombs was told she had until 10:00 p.m. to vacate the house, with the added threat that it would be burned unless Robert Toombs surrendered. "Well, then," Mrs. Toombs replied, "burn it." While the cavalrymen wolfed down the food prepared for the Toombses' supper, Mrs. Toombs and the servants emptied the house of all the belongings they could move. The threat proved an empty one. The next day, Captain Lot Abraham, who had been away from Washington during the attempt to arrest Toombs, apologized to Julia Toombs for the way she had been treated. The arrest of Toombs had been ordered from Washington, D.C. The ceaseless firebrand was high on a list of Rebel leaders that included Davis, Stephens, Toombs and Howell Cobb, all of whom had been politically prominent in national politics before the war. They were now slated for prison. The cavalry sent to arrest Toombs had arrived in Washington from Augusta the day before, and their intent was an open secret.[162]

The nearly full day's warning meant Toombs was not unprepared for the eventual arrival of Yankees at his front door. He had, apparently, made at least rough plans of what he would do. Among the crowd of onlookers to the drama of Julia Toombs's resistance was twenty-one-year-old paroled Confederate artillery lieutenant Charles Edgar Irvin, son of one of Toombs's friends. Irvin almost immediately went to the nearby home of another Toombs friend, J.T. Wingfield, and left notice that Toombs could contact him as to where he should meet Toombs with fresh horses. Early the next morning, he got word to meet Toombs at the farm of John Chennault, about eighteen miles from Washington, in the Danburg community, and to bring his favorite horse, Gray Alice, his mount during his crowded hours of glory at the Battle of Sharpsburg. For the next few months, Toombs and Irvin played a complex game of cat-and-mouse with Federal authorities that relied heavily on Toombs's friends and sympathizers throughout the state.[163]

The two first rode northward for Elbert County, which Toombs had always considered as much home ground as Wilkes County and where he knew he could depend on aid. One of their first hideouts was the island in the Savannah River owned by Alexander Leseur, who was considered locally something of a hermit. Toombs skirted capture when Union cavalry was reportedly tipped by a freed slave in the neighborhood to the presence of some important Confederate on the island. But by the time they closed the net, Toombs was on his way up the Savannah River Valley. Before he left Elbert County, however, he was initiated into a Masonic lodge and took his first degrees. The signs of the order would prove useful to a man on the run.[164]

Toombs and Irvin headed for Habersham County, where Toombs hid out for two weeks at Riverside, the home of Joseph J. Prather on the Tugalo River, while Irvin went back to Washington with letters. During the time Irvin was gone, Toombs had a close call when the hoof beats of Union cavalry thundered across the Prather Bridge, a covered bridge across the Tugalo that faced the house. Prather's wife secreted the rather large Toombs in an upstairs bedroom closet, a hiding place overlooked when the Union troops searched the house. Prather family legend in later years attributed Toombs's escape to the rarity of closets in homes at the time, since closets were considered rooms by tax assessors, and the blue-coated troopers likely thought the door simply connected to the already searched room next door. Toombs, however, supposedly kept two pistols drawn all the while.[165]

It was already early July, and Toombs had been on the run nearly two months. When young Irvin returned to Riverside, he brought word of

Lieutenant William H. Parker, CSN, commandant of the Confederate Naval Academy. His young cadets provided the guard for the Confederate treasury and Richmond bank deposits from Richmond to northeast Georgia. *Courtesy Officers of the Confederacy.*

Joseph Brown's farewell statement. Brown had been arrested in Milledgeville on May 9 after calling a special session of the Georgia legislature to deal with what Brown considered matters of government still in his hands, such as restoring order to the state. Federal authorities considered this a violation of the parole Brown had reluctantly accepted on May 4. He was imprisoned briefly in Washington, D.C., before he was released to return home. His farewell address to the people of Georgia, issued on June 29, dripped with reconciliation to the ears of the adamant Confederate, as it would to Toombs. Of course, slavery should be abolished and the society of Georgia would move on to better times and higher callings, wrote the man who had warned of the terrors of abolition in the fall of 1861.[166] Toombs refused to believe Irvin's report of Brown's address until Irvin handed him a newspaper's account to read himself. "This news," Irvin later recounted, "absolutely sent the old man to bed."[167]

Toombs dispatched Irvin to Savannah to see whether it would be possible to escape through the port. This plan wasn't feasible, Irvin found, and when he returned upriver, he rejoined Toombs at the home of William Rembert, near Tallulah Falls in Rabun County. Toombs was also by now traveling under the name of Luther H.O. Martin, the name of a friend from Elbert County whose parole papers Toombs now carried. Martin had marched away from Elberton in 1861 as the captain of the Fireside Guards, later Company C of the Fifteenth Georgia, but he had resigned in February 1862 and returned to Elbert County and, in March 1864, been elected colonel of one of the county's militia districts. He was also a close associate of William H. Mattox, with whom he would become a partner in a gristmill in November 1865. Toombs and Irvin once again turned south, heading into Elbert County, where Toombs spent at least one night at the home of William H. Mattox, near the home of the authentic Luther Martin. While Toombs was Mattox's guest, according to accounts, Union cavalry raided Martin's home.[168]

The pair turned south again and parted ways in the Centreville community, about twelve miles from Washington, with Toombs telling Irvin where they would next meet, at the home of Linton Stephens in Sparta, Hancock County. The apparent near miss of the Union raid on Martin's home convinced Toombs that capture was only a matter of time if he remained in Georgia. Part of the message Irvin was to carry to Julia was that Toombs would not be able to see her before he fled the country but that he would send for her.[169]

When Irvin rejoined Toombs, the two moved south. Toombs could rely on a huge network of friends, Irvin found, but Toombs was also being recognized more and more frequently, including once by a black man guiding Toombs and Irvin to a plantation in Twiggs County, where their former host had told them they could expect further help. The man had driven his then owner to one of Toombs's speeches seventeen years before, and the voice and Toombs's famous leonine mane had made an impression. It was not problems in remaining hidden that finally turned the pair back toward North Georgia, however; it was their finding that Union cavalry had all the usable ferries across the Ocmulgee River under close watch. They remained dodging around the North Georgia hills until October before turning south again. This time, in Washington County, they managed to cross the Ocmulgee River. When Toombs suspected the ferryman recognized him, he directed Irvin to offer the man money. The ferryman refused, saying, "Tell General Toombs I wish to God I could do something for him."[170]

Toombs was the last of the Union forces' most wanted, and the pursuit had not cooled. In early August, Julia Toombs had queried General J.B. Steedman in Augusta whether Toombs could be paroled if he gave himself up. Joseph Brown had even made a pitch that Toombs, as a general in the state forces since he had resigned from the Confederate army, was covered by the blanket parole Brown had signed as the state forces' commander-in-chief. When Steedman cabled the War Department, back came a firm reply from Secretary of War Edwin Stanton: By the President Andrew Johnson's order, if Toombs surrendered to Union forces, he would be arrested and held at Fort Warren.

It wasn't capture, a trial, prison or even death that he feared, Toombs confided to Irvin in bits and pieces as the two men rode together for most of seven months. It was being made a spectacle as a captive—the great Robert Toombs exhibited like an animal in a zoo. He would not be taken alive. The two spent some time at Toombs's plantation in Stewart County and then crossed into Alabama, reaching Mobile. There Toombs stayed while Irvin traveled to New Orleans in hopes of securing from the Spanish consul a pass for "Luther Martin" to enter Cuba. On the run, Toombs had often spread the rumor that he was already in Cuba and now he planned to actually go there. On Irvin's return, the two booked on a packet boat for New Orleans, from where Toombs sailed for Cuba on November 5. Against Irvin's warning, he insisted on remaining on deck before the ship sailed. "I want fresh air, and I will die right here," he told Irvin. "I am impatient to get into neutral waters so I can talk. I have not had a square, honest talk in six months." Without his talk, he wasn't Robert Toombs.[171]

From Havana on December 15, he wrote Stephens. Toombs took umbrage at those like Joseph Brown who were now seeking to cooperate with the occupying forces, saying that the war had settled the political issues. "How can war settle anything except which is the strongest party to the pending contest?" As for himself, he planned to stay well out of reach of the U.S. government. If the politics called for it, he wrote Stephens, a military tribunal could hang him with more justice than Mary Surratt, hanged that July in Washington, D.C., for an alleged role in Lincoln's assassination. "For I did try to take the life of the nation," he said, "and I sorely regret the failure to do it."[172]

On May 8, William Crump left Washington for Richmond. One of the first actions after the Union cavalry rode into Washington was the seizure of the Richmond bank specie as suspected Confederate government funds. Crump, on the advice of Garnett Andrews, intended to go to Richmond and establish the money as the banks' holdings. A few days later, on May 18, four agents of the banks arrived in Washington with documents releasing the gold for return to Virginia. After consultation with Andrews, the bankers prepared to move the specie overland, essentially along the route by which it had reached Washington.[173]

Early on the morning of May 24, four wagons carrying the gold, with the bankers and a twelve-man cavalry escort of the Washington garrison, rolled

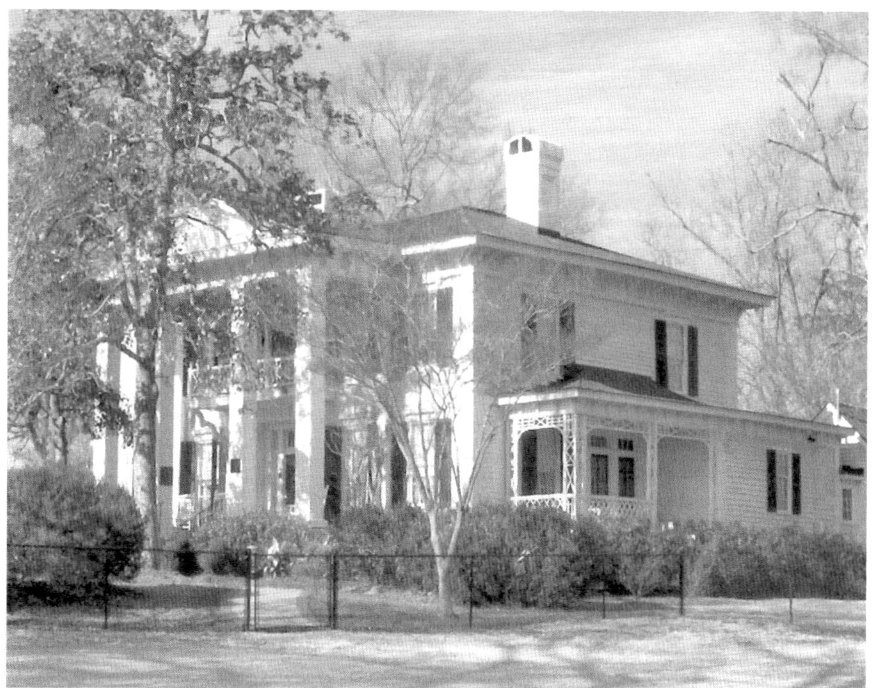

The Burt-Starke House, Abbeville, South Carolina. Davis held his last council of war here the night before he crossed into Georgia.

out of Washington. It was probably no secret to anyone in town what the wagons carried, and that was to prove fatal.

By nightfall, the wagons had reached the home of William Moss, near the Danburg community, eighteen miles from Washington, where the party went into camp. According to later testimony, two members of the Moss family rode across the yard near midnight, and later a soldier who appeared to be wearing a U.S. Army coat rode into view, appeared to look over the scene and then vanished into the dark.

About midnight, the camp was rushed by an estimated twenty to twenty-five men carrying cavalry carbines and pistols. The teamsters fled, and the escort cavalrymen offered no fight to the raiders. The robbers smashed open the boxes of coins and opened the sacks. They poured coins into saddlebags and haversacks, taking little care not to spill any as they filled everything they could. The spilled coins, according to one witness, were ankle deep. And as quickly as they came, they were gone, leaving trails of dropped coins behind them. One dropped his whole overloaded haversack as it ripped open.[171]

The bankers later claimed the robbers were of the Seventh and Eighth Tennessee Cavalry, Union regiments, but at least one ex-Confederate laid the robbery at the comrades' feet. Lewis Shepherd, of Vaughn's Brigade of Tennesseans, which had been with Davis's cavalry escort, wrote years later that some men of Vaughn's Brigade "became apprised that a train of specie was being carried north under Federal escort, and they jumped to the conclusion that it was the property of the Confederate government which the Federals had captured."[175]

The men, Shepherd wrote, decided to take the money and had stalked the wagon train all day looking for a chance to raid it. "They charged the train, captured and disarmed the guard, and proceeded at once to knock the heads out of the kegs and the lids off the boxes containing the gold and fill their forage sacks with ten- and twenty-dollar gold pieces." Shepherd claimed to know several of the raiders personally (without implicating himself) and claimed that several went west and used their loot as the start of greater fortunes.

In the light of morning, the bankers collected what money was left, nearly $160,000, and one banker, John M. Goddin, continued on with the specie to the railhead at Abbeville, South Carolina. The other bankers organized a search for the raiders and the money, offering rewards for the robbers and recovery of the money. In Washington, Porter Alexander formed a posse of about fourteen men, mainly members of the local Irwin Artillery, with a local magistrate, Judge William Reese, along with warrants, and rode for Danburg. "We came upon a part of guerillas [*sic*] who had about $80,000 of the money in charge," Alexander recalled years afterward. "They said they did not know it was private property; believing it to belong to the Confederacy, they thought they were as much entitled to it as anyone else... but being convinced it was private property, they were willing to surrender it." The confrontation took place with pistols drawn, but there were no shots fired. In all, Alexander and his party recovered about $110,000, including about $10,000 found hidden among local slaves. The money was returned to the Bank of Georgia vault.[176]

EVEN BEFORE THE RAID on the treasure wagons, locals saw signs that the remnants of their old society the war had left them were slipping away. Travelers from Augusta reported around the Andrews table that freed blacks were crowding into the town. Without any means of supporting themselves, some expected the Union forces to feed them. But that was not forthcoming, and then they found their former owners either would not or could not take responsibility for them. Another guest had tried to reach Clarkesville, in Habersham County, but had turned back because the countryside was overrun by roving gangs of thieves and robbers. The women having business in Clarkesville had dared go no farther than Athens. "The Yankees have committed so many depredations there that the whole country is destitute and the people are desperate," Eliza Andrews observed. "The poor are clamoring for bread and many of them have taken to bushwhacking as their only means of living."

On the evening of May 18, word spread of a column of Union cavalry storming down the road from Greensboro, southwest of Washington, looting anything that pleased them. The Andrewses hid their silver in a prepared space in the chimney, and Garnett Andrews loaded two guns. Even being known to have no Confederate sympathies no longer offered the slight protection it once had. The column rode through Washington, but the Andrewses were not bothered. The next day, Eliza heard the column had been bushwhacked outside Greensboro, with a few of the men killed. She surmised they had lost their taste for looting by the time they reached Washington.[177]

On May 24, the same morning the wagons loaded with the Richmond banks' gold slipped out of town just before dawn, the Lot Abraham and the Fourth Iowa garrison left town, headed for Augusta, giving no indications that other bluecoats would be taking their place. "They were much disgusted with their reception here, I am told," Eliza recalled, "and some of them were heard to declare there was not a pretty woman in the place." It didn't puzzle Eliza why members of the garrison had wanted for companionship among the wilted flowers of Washington's young womanhood. The only ones who had associated with them were the newly freed black girls. "They had two negro balls while they were here, the white men dancing with the negro women…They strutted about the streets on Sundays as women…They strutted about the streets on Sundays with negro wenches on their arms, and yet their officers complain because they are not invited to sit at the tables of Southern gentlemen!" The next day, though, Eliza had second thoughts. "They say it is not safe for a person to go six miles from town except in company and fully armed, and I am not sure we are going to be safe in the village, the negroes are crowding in so. 'Marse' Abraham did protect us from them, in a way, and if his men hadn't tampered with them so, I shouldn't be sorry to see them back till things settle down a bit." Abraham and his men did return later, joined by others.[178]

Brigadier General Edward A. Wild, acting assistant commissioner of the Freedmen's Bureau for the area that included Washington, originally came to Washington to investigate a murder. Two young men were accused of beating to death an elderly black woman who had wanted to leave the plantation where she had lived most of her life. They had asked Garnett Andrews to defend them. Wild, though, soon lost interest in the case when stories of stolen gold reached his ears. He had already, soon after reaching Washington, played a part in having the Richmond bankers still in town arrested and their funds in the Bank of Georgia's vault seized.

The Massachusetts-born Wild was a Harvard-trained doctor who had nevertheless opted for a field commission when the war began instead of entering the medical corps. Over the course of the war, the reasons would become clear: the rabid abolitionist hated Southerners with an unconcealed passion, and on the battlefield was where he could best hand out their punishment. His hatred was, if anything, stoked to a white heat by his empty left sleeve, a relic of wounds suffered in September 1862 at the fighting at South Mountain, Maryland, that preceded the Battle of Sharpsburg. So it was with eager ears that he listened when, in mid-July, a former slave of John Chennault, at whose home Toombs had first met Charles Irvin with fresh horses, reached Wild's headquarters with a tale that both John Chennault and his brother Dionysius had not only taken part in the raid on the wagons but were hiding much of the missing money. With this woman, Angelina, in tow, Wild and his picked unit of cavalrymen rode the eighteen miles to the Danburg community.

The first act of the bluecoats was to kill the Chennaults' dog, according to accounts, shooting and bayoneting the animals, "laughing and hoorahing" as they ignored the cries of the Chennault children. Wild immediately arrested the two brothers, as well as John's son Frank, and he and his men immediately set about torturing the whereabouts of the missing money out of them. The Chennaults were herded into a nearby woodlot, where, according to a later account by Mary Ann Chennault Shumate, seventeen at the time, "they tied them up with their hands behind them and hung them up by their thumbs, with their feet off the ground. They said that after the first time they begged the Yankees to shoot them dead rather than to suffer so again…There [*sic*] hands were so black and swelled up that it was a long time before they could use them again." The torture went on for the rest of the day and the night. When torturing the white men proved fruitless, Wild ordered the torture of John Chennault's body servant, Tom, who happened to be Angelina's son.[179]

Others of Wild's command, plus the busy Angelina, were heaping insults on the Chennault women. "Some of the soldiers came to the house and began cursing and abusing Ma and the children," Mary Ann Chennault Shumate recalled. "They took Ma and me and Aunt Deasy [Mrs. Dionysius Chennault] and shut us up in a room and forced us to strip off all our clothes while Angelina came in and searched us." Nothing was found on the women. And nothing was wrung out of the men. All Wild could seize was some few pieces of jewelry the Chennault women had and $150 in coins belonging to the brothers. But all six Chennaults—the two brothers, their wives, Mary Ann and Frank—were taken back to Washington and jailed.

The Chennaults remained jailed for some days while Garnett Andrews traveled to Augusta to plead their case before Wild's superior, Major General James Steedman. Andrews returned with Colonel E.L. Drayton of Steedman's staff. "Colonel Drayton behaved very generously and sent us back home just as soon as he could finish investigating the case," recalled Mary Ann Chennault Shumate. He also returned the Chennaults' property and freed the Richmond bankers. But he didn't free their money.

Wild during the same period had also evicted Julia Toombs from her home, using it as his headquarters and declaring his intent to use it as a

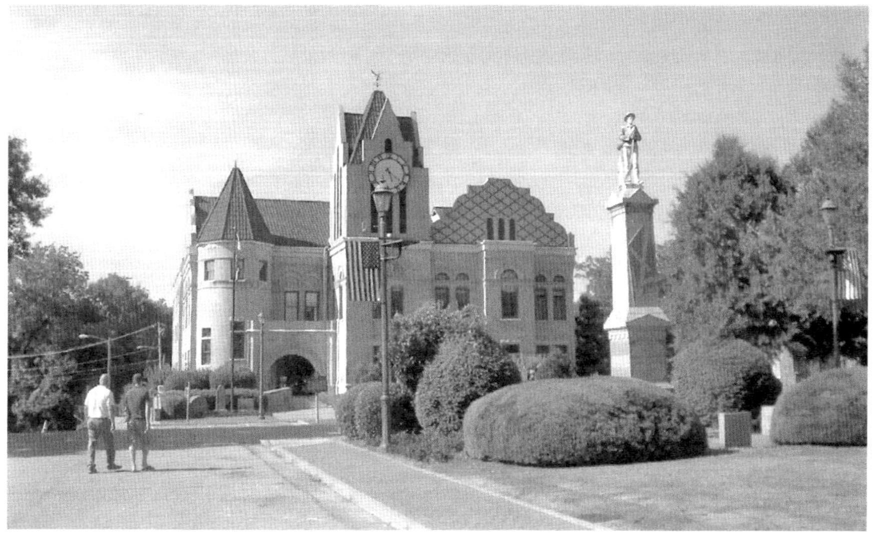

Where the Wilkes County Courthouse now stands on the square in Washington, the Bank of Georgia building once stood. There, Jefferson Davis held his last cabinet meeting. *Author's photograph.*

school for black children. He was recalled to Augusta, however, before he realized any of these plans and shipped off to another post. Before he left Augusta, a gunman tried to kill him, bursting into his office with a revolver and unleashing a fusillade of shots. Another officer was shot, but Wild emerged unscathed. The gunman was never identified.[130]

Epilogue

The Civil War in northeast Georgia ground to a halt at some vague point in the spring or early summer of 1865. It could be said it happened at different times for different people, when the reality of defeat set in. The region was the last part of the main Confederacy to feel the direct hand of the war that the politicians of the area had done so much to start.

With two exceptions—William McIntosh and Thomas R.R. Cobb—all the central people whose stories added a brushstroke to the war years in northeast Georgia survived the fighting.

Singleton McIntosh, twenty at the war's end, returned home from the Seventh Georgia Cavalry, with which he had served in Virginia for most of the war. In December 1864, he had been one of a contingent sent back to Georgia for fresh horses. Most of the men of this unit had been in North Carolina, on the way back to the Army of Northern Virginia, when they learned of the surrender at Appomattox Courthouse. He took over the operation of what remained of his father's plantation and, in following years, became a prosperous farmer. He died in November 1908 and lies buried near his father.

Howell Cobb surrendered in Macon on April 20, 1865, and was paroled, despite first intentions to arrest him. He returned to Athens, rebuilt his law practice and began seeking a presidential pardon. When he received it in early 1868, he immediately began a series of speeches denouncing the Reconstruction policies. In the fall of that year, he went to New York to speak and died there of a heart attack on October 9.

Alexander H. Stephens was released from prison in October 1865, after only five months. In 1866, he was elected to the U.S. Senate from Georgia but was prevented from taking his seat because of his Confederate past. At home in Crawfordville, he wrote a constitutional defense of the South's secession. In 1873, he was elected to the U.S. House of Representatives and reelected to four more terms. He resigned on November 4, 1882, because he had been elected governor of Georgia. He would serve only four months, however, dying in March 1883. In the years after the war, his ailments had wracked him with increasing pain, which he handled with increasing amounts of alcohol and opiates. He and Toombs were never at odds again and remained the closest of friends.

Joseph Brown continued his pursuit of the main chance. He prospered financially during the Reconstruction years, joining with the Republican Reconstruction government, and was in 1868 appointed chief justice of the Georgia supreme court. By the time he died in 1894, it is estimated his net worth was greater than $1 million. Almost to a man, his former Confederate comrades despised him—Toombs, perhaps, above all.

Edward Porter Alexander went on to a career in railroading and banking but never lost his love of engineering. He wrote his personal memoirs of his war years while on a project in Nicaragua in the late 1890s, a few years before he died in Savannah.

Garnett Andrews, despite his steadfast Unionist views, found little favor in the Reconstruction South. His seeking of appointments as a federal district attorney or judge met with failure. He was, however, appointed a state court judge, a position he held until his death in 1873.

Following her father's death, Eliza Andrews, then thirty-three years old and unmarried, had nothing to keep her in Washington. She took a teaching job in Yazoo City, Mississippi, for a year before becoming the superintendent of the Washington Girls' Academy back home for six years. She joined the faculty of Wesleyan College in Macon in 1885 and taught rhetoric and history until 1898. She taught botany at Washington High School until she retired in 1903. Andrews published three novels and two textbooks on botany. Politically active, she identified herself as a socialist. A few years before her death in 1931, she was voted a member of the International Academy of Science.

E.H. Sutton was captured on July 2, 1863, at Gettysburg and was held prisoner until he was exchanged in February 1865. After returning home to Habersham County on forty days' leave, he was in North Carolina, on his way back to the army, when he learned of Lee's surrender. He simply turned south again for home. He took his parole in Hartwell, Georgia, in late April 1865. He returned to Habersham County. In 1907, he published his memoirs.

Warren Akins also sought his parole in Hartwell via a letter hand-carried by Amos T. Akerman. Akins returned to Cassville and rebuilt his home and his law practice. He died in Cartersville in 1877.

Amos T. Akerman, the New Hampshire–born Elbertonian, became active in the Freedmen's Bureau in Georgia. During the presidency of Ulysses S. Grant, Akerman served for a time as U.S. attorney general and was very active in prosecuting the Ku Klux Klan.

Julia Toombs joined Robert in Havana in December 1865. They went to Paris, though Julia later returned to Washington. In October 1866, Toombs's last surviving child, his daughter Sallie, died in Washington. "This blow is insupportable," he wrote Stephens. "It has crushed my heart and buried my hopes in the grave." Brokenhearted and weary of life abroad, he decided to return to Georgia in early 1867. "The worst that can happen to me is prison," he wrote Julia, who had returned home before he did, "and I don't see much to choose between my present condition and any decent fort."

After his return, Toombs traveled to Washington, D.C., where he had an interview with President Andrew Johnson. Apparently, the interview ended whatever thoughts Johnson might have had of having the former Confederate officer and government official arrested. Toombs returned home to Georgia and was never molested by federal authorities again.

Yet Toombs never applied for a pardon. "I am not loyal to the existing government of the United States and do not wish to be suspected of loyalty," he proclaimed. He resumed his law practice with his son-in-law, Dudley Dubose, specializing in railroad cases, and his income soon reached an estimated $40,000 per year. He remained active in banking, railroads and politics.

Toombs favored adopting a new state constitution to replace the one ratified by the Reconstruction government in 1868, calling it a "nigger constitution constructed by knaves and carpet baggers." At rallies, he urged crowds, "I can make you a constitution by which the people will rule and the nigger will never be heard from." The statements only served to further galvanize northern Republicans and vexed southern and northern Democrats who hoped the Democrat candidate might win the presidency in 1876. The Georgia General Assembly hastily declared it had no intention of disenfranchising blacks.

Nevertheless, a new state constitution was ratified in 1877, and Toombs emerged from the debate a populist hero, having helped craft a constitution that dealt with state aid to railroads, regulation of railroad tariffs and taxation of corporations. As it turned out, this would be his final hurrah in the public arena.

By 1883, Toombs had lost the two people he held most dear: his beloved Julia and his lifelong friend Stephens. Afterward, according to acquaintances, Toombs's drinking increased, and he seldom left home. In the words of one observer, "He deliberately chose to drain bitter cups of purpose to sweeten bitter memories…During this time he was dying by inches."

Robert Toombs died on December 15, 1885, in Washington, ending a talented but tumultuous life. One of the clergy officiating at his funeral was Granby Hillyer, whom Toombs had assaulted sixty years before during their university days. The *Atlanta Constitution* noted that the day was "calm and bright, in strange contrast with [Toombs's] stormy life." The storm had finally blown out, and an unnatural quiet settled over Washington for the first time in some seventy years.

William H. Mattox continued to thrive after the war. By the late 1880s, he had served a term in the legislature and had amassed over three thousand acres along the upper Savannah River Valley that he worked with convicts leased from the state. He acquired a reputation for almost sadistic cruelty toward them. In June 1889, he hosted Atlanta newspaper editor Henry W. Grady, by then well established as the voice of the New South, to a barbecue and gala in Elberton to kick off a new venture Mattox and partners were starting: the county's first cotton spinning mill. Grady, already famous for his "New South" speech in New York City three years earlier, gave another speech that has made the anthologies, on the southern farmer. Mattox's mill adventures proved less successful. A fire from a bolt of lightning burned the uninsured mill, and Mattox was nearly ruined. He was killed in a gun battle with his son-in-law in 1900. They were arguing over a horse.

The most prolific of the cast in putting pen to paper in the postwar years, Porter Alexander and Eliza Andrews, pondered the meaning of the heady and dreadful years.

The right to secede, Alexander wrote in his memoirs, had never been in doubt. "We had the right therefore to secede whenever we saw fit, & it was truly for our liberty that we fought. Slavery brought up the discussion of the right in Congress & in the press, but the South would never have united as it did in secession & in war had [the right] not been generally denied at the North & particularly by the Republican Party."

In defeat, Alexander wrote, the South was vindicated by demonstrated courage and brilliant victories. In the end, however, he said, "each side may take equal pride in Lee who surrendered & in Grant who rose to the occasion by giving such honorable & generous terms."

In the introduction to her wartime diary, published in 1908, Eliza Andrews strikes a more poignant note, maybe in part a product of her experiences on the Confederate homefront. While holding dear the memories of the brave Southerners who had fought and hoping future generations of Southerners revered them and were inspired by them, she recounted an anecdote of an aged Confederate soldier standing at the site where many in blue and gray had fought and died. The old man felt his sorrows for both, "all brothers once more."

"That is the sentiment of the New South and of the few of us who survive from the old," she wrote. "We look back with loving memory upon our past, as we look upon the grave of the beloved dead whom we mourn but would not recall."

Notes

Chapter 1

1. McIntosh, *Official History of Elbert County*, 117–18.
2. Burton, *Extraordinary*, 8–14.
3. McIntosh, *Official History of Elbert County*, 114–15.
4. Ibid., 117–18.
5. Ibid., 112.
6. Ibid., 108; U.S. Census Data for 1860—Elbert County; Will of William M. McIntosh, probated November 1862.
7. U.S. Census Data for 1860—Elbert County.
8. Andrews, *Wartime Journal*, 177–78; U.S. Census Data for Wilkes County.
9. Andrews, *Wartime Journal*, 178.
10. Alexander, *Fighting for the Confederacy*, 21.
11. Ibid., 23–25.
12. Ibid., 554(n).
13. Coleman, *Confederate Athens*, 31, 3–4.
14. Davis, *Union That Shaped the Confederacy*, 76–80.
15. Coleman, *Confederate Athens*, 28.
16. Ibid., 17–21.
17. Ibid., 21.
18. Ibid., 22.
19. Ibid., 26–27.
20. Ibid., 31.

21. Ibid., 33–36; Davis, *Henry Grady's New South*, 29–30.
22. Sarris, *Separate Civil War*, 22, 58–59.
23. Sutton, *Civil War Stories*, 1–5.
24. Ibid., 6–10.
25. Ibid., 10.
26. McIntosh, *Official History of Elbert County*, 115.
27. Ibid., 126.

Chapter 2

28. Johnson, *Toward a Patriarchal Republic*, 5–6.
29. Ibid., 63–64.
30. Ibid., 64.
31. Davis, *Union That Shaped the Confederacy*, 37–40.
32. Morotta and Russell, "Protective Tariffs."
33. Heidler, *Pulling the Temple Down*, 167–68.
34. Johnson, *Toward a Patriarchal Republic*, 198.
35. Freehling and Simpson, eds., *Secession Debated*, 4.
36. Johnson, *Toward a Patriarchal Republic*, 201; DeCredico, *Patriotism for Profit*, 7–10.
37. Johnson, *Toward a Patriarchal Republic*, 6–15.
38. Schott, *Alexander H. Stephens*, 125–29.
39. Davis, *Union That Shaped the Confederacy*, 60–64.
40. Mohr, *On the Threshold of Freedom*, 20–22, 40.
41. Ibid., 21.
42. Ibid., 6.
43. Ibid., 44.
44. Ibid., 14–15.
45. Ibid, p. 11
46. Johnson, *Toward a Patriarchal Republic*, 45.
47. Schott, *Alexander H. Stephens*, 233–36.
48. Ibid., 233–34.
49. Chandler, "Rebel Lion," 21–22.
50. Ibid., 22.
51. Ibid., 23.
52. Ibid.
53. Ibid., 24.
54. Ibid.

55. Ibid., 25.
56. Ibid., 25–26.
57. Johnson, *Toward a Patriarchal Republic*, 17.
58. Freehling and Simpson, eds., *Secession Debated*, 3–5.
59. Davis, *Union That Shaped the Confederacy*, 99–104; Johnson, *Toward a Patriarchal Republic*, 16.
60. Freehling and Simpson, eds., *Secession Debated*, 6–7.
61. Ibid., 9.
62. Davis, *Union That Shaped the Confederacy*, 4.
63. Freehling and Simpson, eds., *Secession Debated*, 52–79.
64. Johnson, *Toward a Patriarchal Republic*, 49–50.
65. Williams, et al, *Plain Folk*, 11–12.
66. Johnson, *Toward a Patriarchal Republic*, 116–17.
67. Williams, et al, *Plain Folk*, 14; *Georgia's Secession Convention*, online source, docsouth.unc.edu/imls/georgia/georgia.html, for breakdown of votes.
68. Sarris, *Separate Civil War*, 49–51.

Chapter 3

69. Coleman, *Confederate Athens*, 160.
70. Ibid., 97–98.
71. Williams, et al, *Plain Folk*, 35.
72. Ibid., 34–35; Coleman, *Confederate Athens*, 81.
73. Coleman, *Confederate Athens*, 82.
74. Williams, et al, *Plain Folk*, 63; McIntosh, *Official History of Elbert County*, 122.
75. Coleman, *Confederate Athens*, 160–61.
76. Ibid., 163.
77. Andrews, *Footsteps of a Regiment*, 38.
78. Chandler, "Toombs at Burnside Bridge."
79. Coleman, *Confederate Athens*, 164.
80. Ibid., 165.
81. Erwin, "Stoneman's Raid."
82. Coleman, *Confederate Athens*, 169–70.
83. Ibid., 171.
84. Evans, *Sherman's Horsemen*, 347.
85. Ibid., 347–48.
86. Coleman, *Confederate Athens*, 170–71.
87. Evans, *Sherman's Horsemen*, 348–52.

88. Coleman, *Confederate Athens*, 171.
89. Sarris, *Separate Civil War*, 89.
90. Ibid., 87.
91. Ibid., 90.
92. Dorsey, *History of Hall County*, 163–64.
93. Williams, et al, *Plain Folk*, 162; Coleman, *Confederate Athens*, 166.
94. *Official Records of the War of the Rebellion*, series 99, vol. 4 Operations in NC, SC, GA and East FLA, p. 1092.
95. Williams, et al, *Plain Folk*, 94.
96. Ibid., 95.
97. Ibid., 103.
98. *Official Records*, series 4, part 2, 126–31.
99. Williams, et al, *Plain Folk*, 96.
100. Ibid., 121.
101. Ibid., 120.
102. Ibid., 130.
103. *Southern Watchman*, February 15, 1865.
104. New Georgia Encyclopedia, "William T. Wofford." www.georgiaencyclopedia.org/articles/history-archaeology/w-t-wofford-1824-1884.
105. *Southern Banner*, January 18, 1865.
106. Williams, et al, *Plain Folk*, 185.
107. *Southern Watchman*, January 18, 1865.
108. *Southern Banner*, March 22, 1865.
109. Williams, et al, *Plain Folk*, 85.
110. *Southern Watchman*, April 12, 1865.
111. Wiley, ed., *Letters of Warren Akin*, 6–7.
112. Ibid., 7.
113. Andrew, "Essential Nationalism of the People," 128–31.
114. Wiley, ed., *Letters of Warren Akin*, 34.
115. Ibid., 34.
116. Ibid., 120, 122.
117. Mohr, *On the Threshold of Freedom*, 205–6.
118. Ibid., 205.
119. Ibid., 198.
120. Ibid., 205, 211.
121. Ibid., 220.
122. Ibid., 226.
123. Wiley, ed., *Letters of Warren Akin*, 74.

124. Ibid., 69.
125. Chandler, "Meanest Man in Georgia," 44.
126. Ibid., 45.
127. Ibid., 46.

Chapter 4

128. Andrews, *Wartime Journal*, 154–72.
129. Ibid., 159.
130. Ibid., 173.
131. Jackman, *Diary of a Confederate Soldier*, 166.
132. Ibid., 167.
133. Ibid., 167–68.
134. Andrews, *Wartime Journal*, 194.
135. Jackman, *Diary of a Confederate Soldier*, 167.
136. Andrews, *Wartime Journal*, 199.
137. Ibid., 188.
138. Ibid., 184, 199–200.
139. Ibid., 189.
140. Davis, "Vanished Civil War Gold," 39.
141. Parker, *Recollections of a Naval Officer*, 373.
142. Ibid., 378; *Official Records*, series 1, Vol. 3, 545–547, "The Pursuit and Capture of Jefferson Davis."
143. Parker, *Recollections of a Naval Officer*, 378.
144. Ibid., 282–83.
145. Ibid., 288.
146. Davis, *Long Surrender*, 122–26.
147. Ibid., 122–23.
148. Jackman, *Diary of a Confederate Soldier*, 167.
149. Andrews, *Wartime Journal*, 202.
150. Ibid., 204.
151. Davis, *Long Surrender*, 115.
152. Ibid., 128–29; Andrews, *Wartime Journal*, 205.
153. Alexander, *Fighting for the Confederacy*, 532.
154. Ibid., 547–52.
155. Jackman, *Diary of a Confederate Soldier*, 168.
156. Andrews, *Wartime Journal*, 219–20.
157. Ibid., 230–31.

158. Blackwell, *1865 Stoneman's Raid Ends*, 109–12.
159. *Recollections of the United Daughters of the Confederacy*, 576–77.
160. Scott and Angel, *History of the Twelfth Tennessee Volunteer Cavalry*, 242.
161. *Atlanta Constitution*, August 29, 1877.
162. Andrews, *Wartime Journal*, 242–43.
163. Stovall, *Robert Toombs*, 288.
164. Ibid., 288–89.
165. *Anderson Independent-Mail*, May 21, 2014.
166. Parks, *Joseph E. Brown*, 327–29, 334.
167. Stovall, *Robert Toombs*, 290.
168. Ibid., 291–92.
169. Ibid., 292.
170. Ibid., 293–97.
171. Ibid., 302–5.
172. Phillips, *Life of Robert Toombs*, 255.
173. Andrews, *Wartime Journal*, 229; Davis, "Vanished Civil War Gold," 40.
174. Davis, "Vanished Civil War Gold," 40–41.
175. Willingham, *History of Wilkes County*, 177–78.
176. Ibid., 178.
177. Andrews, *Wartime Journal*, 261–264.
178. Ibid., 267–68.
179. Chandler, "Mystery of the Gold," 43.
180. Ibid., 44.

Bibliography

Newspapers

Anderson Independent-Mail
Southern Banner
Southern Watchman

Books and Publications

Alexander, Edward Porter. *Fighting for the Confederacy.* Edited by Gary W. Gallagher. Chapel Hill: University of North Carolina Press, 1989.

Andrew, Rod. "The Essential Nationalism of the People: Georgia's Confederate Congressional Elections of 1863." In *Inside the Confederate Nation*, edited by Lesley Gordon and John Inscoe. Baton Rouge: Louisiana State University Press, 2005.

Andrews, Eliza Frances. *The Wartime Journal of a Georgia Girl, 1864–1865.* Lincoln: University of Nebraska Press, 1997.

Andrews, W.H. *Footsteps of a Regiment.* Atlanta: Longstreet Press, 1992.

Blackwell, Joshua Beau. *The 1865 Stoneman's Raid Ends.* Charleston, SC: The History Press, 2011.

Burton, Brian K. *Extraordinary Circumstances: The Seven Days Battles.* Bloomington: Indiana University Press, 2001.

Chandler, Ray. "The Meanest Man in Georgia." *Georgia Backroads Magazine* (Fall 2012).

———. "The Mystery of the Gold at Chennault's Crossing." *North Georgia Journal* (Winter 1998).

———. "Rebel Lion." *Georgia Backroads Magazine* (Spring 2008).

———. "Toombs at Burnside Bridge." *Georgia Backroads Magazine* (Summer 2007).

Coleman, Kenneth. *Confederate Athens*. Athens: University of Georgia Press, 2009.

Davis, Burke. *The Long Surrender*. New York: Vintage Books, 1985.

Davis, Harold E. *Henry Grady's New South*. Birmingham: University of Alabama Press, 1990.

Davis, Robert. "Vanished Civil War Gold." *North Georgia Journal* (Summer 1999).

Davis, William C. *The Union That Shaped the Confederacy: Robert Toombs & Alexander H. Stephens*. Lincoln: University Press of Nebraska, 2001.

DeCredico, Mary. *Patriotism for Profit*. Chapel Hill: University of North Carolina Press, 1990.

Dorsey, James. *The History of Hall County*. Vol. 1, *1818–1900*. Gainesville, GA: Magnolia Press, n.d.

Erwin, Goodloe. "Stoneman's Raid and the Battle of Barber Creek." Presentation to Athens Historical Society, March 20, 2005.

Evans, David. *Sherman's Horsemen*. Bloomington: Indiana University Press, 1996.

Freehling, William, and Craig Simpson, eds. *Secession Debated: Georgia's Showdown in 1860*. Oxford, UK: Oxford University Press, 1992.

Heidler, David S. *Pulling the Temple Down: The Fire-Eaters and the Destruction of the Union*. Mechanicsburg, PA: Stackpole Books, 1994.

Jackman, John S. *Diary of a Confederate Soldier*. Edited by William C. Davis. Athens: University of Georgia Press, 1990.

Johnson, Michael P. *Toward a Patriarchal Republic: Secession in Georgia*. Baton Rouge: University of Louisiana Press, 1977.

McIntosh, John. *The Official History of Elbert County, 1790–1935*. Elbert County, GA: Stephen Heard Chapter of the Daughters of the American Revolution, 1940.

Mohr, Clarence. *On the Threshold of Freedom: Masters and Slaves in Civil War Georgia*. Baton Rouge: Louisiana State University Press, 1986.

Morotta, David John, and Megan Russell. "Protective Tariffs: Primary Cause of the Civil War?" Paper submitted to *Journal of Economic History* (Fall 2006).

Parker, William H. *Recollections of a Naval Officer, 1841–1865*. 1882. Repr., Annapolis, MD: Naval Institute Press, 1995.

Parks, Joseph H. *Joseph E. Brown of Georgia*. Baton Rouge: Louisiana State University Press, 1977.

Phillips, Ulrich Bancell. *The Life of Robert Toombs*. New York: Macmillan Company, 1913.

Recollections of the United Daughters of the Confederacy. Robert A. Thomas Chapter, Westminster S.C. Vol. 1, 1966.

Sarris, Jonathan Dean. *A Separate Civil War*. Charlottesville: University of Virginia Press, 2006.

Schott, Thomas E. *Alexander H. Stephens: A Biography*. Baton Rouge: Louisiana State University Press, 1988.

Scott, Samuel, and Samuel Angel. *History of the Twelfth Tennessee Volunteer Cavalry*. N.p.: P.F Ziegler and Son, 1905.

Stovall, Pleasant A. *Robert Toombs: Statesman, Speaker, Soldier, Sage*. New York: Cassell Publishing, 1892.

Sutton, E.H. *Civil War Stories*. N.p.: privately published, 1910.

Wiley, Bell Irwin, ed. *Letters of Warren Akin, Confederate Congressman*. Athens: University of Georgia Press, 1959.

Williams, David, et al. *Plain Folk in a Rich Man's War*. Gainesville: University of Florida Press, 2002.

Willingham, Robert M. *The History of Wilkes County*. Washington, GA: Wilkes Publishing Co., 2002.

Compilations

Official Records of the War of the Rebellion, series 99, vol. 4. Operations in North Carolina, South Carooina, Georgia and east Florida. Washington, D.C.: Government Printing Office, 1882.

Index

G

H

I

J

K

L

M

N

O

P

R

S

T

U

V

W

About the Author

Ray Chandler is a journalist and freelance writer from Elberton, Georgia. His work has appeared in the *Athens Banner-Herald*, the *Atlanta Journal-Constitution* and various magazines, including *Georgia Backroads*. For the last ten years he has been a correspondent with Scripps News, covering politics, legal matters and crime. American and British history, and especially the history of Georgia, have been lifelong passions.